ADVANCED PREPARATION FOR THE DIGITAL SAT® EXAM

ACHIEVE A 1550+ SCORE, GET INTO THE COLLEGE OF YOUR DREAMS, AND UNLOCK TOP SCHOLARSHIPS! YOUR COMPLETE PREP WITH 5 FULL-LENGTH PRACTICE TESTS INCLUDED

PREP MASTER ACADEMY

TABLE OF CONTENT

CHAPTER 1: OVERVIEW

EXAM STRUCTURE AND FEATURES

The Digital SAT® is a substantial departure from the traditional paper-based SAT®, reflecting the larger digital change of education. This chapter looks into the details of the exam's format, duration, covered subjects, and authorized instruments, offering a thorough understanding required for efficient preparation.

The Digital SAT® is precisely designed to evaluate a wide range of skills, resulting in a comprehensive assessment of a student's preparation for college-level work. The exam is organized into two major sections: Math and Reading & Writing, each with two modules. The test is unique in that it is adaptive, with the difficulty of questions in the second module influenced by the student's performance in the first.

Math Section

The math component assesses a student's aptitude for using mathematical ideas to solve practical issues. It includes questions on complex math subjects, algebra, geometry, and data analysis. This component evaluates not only rote memorizing of formulas, but also a thorough comprehension of mathematical ideas and applications.

The section is divided into two modules:

- **Module 1**: This module presents questions of varying difficulty levels. It acts as a diagnostic tool to determine the level of competency of the learner.
- **Module 2**: Based on the performance in Module 1, Module 2 adjusts the difficulty level of questions. A strong performance in the first module leads to more challenging questions in the second, which are worth more points.

Reading & Writing Section

The Reading & Writing part assesses students' comprehension, critical thinking, and writing abilities. Unlike the old SAT®, which divided these skills into different portions, the Digital SAT® combines them into a single format that reflects the intricacies of real-world reading and writing activities.

The section is structured as follows:

- **Module 1**: Similar to the Math section, this module includes a mix of question difficulties to establish a baseline for the student.
- **Module 2**: Adaptively adjusts to present questions that align with the student's demonstrated abilities in Module 1.

Exam Duration

The Digital SAT® has a total duration of about two hours, which is much shorter than the prior three-hour paper version. With so little time, students must be both efficient and productive in their test-taking procedures.

Each segment (Math, Reading, and Writing) is allowed a specified amount of time, with small intervals in between. Because the test is adaptive, students must carefully manage their time inside each module, as they cannot return to prior questions after submitting a module.

- *Math Section*: 70 minutes (35 minutes per module)
- *Reading & Writing Section*: 80 minutes (40 minutes per module)

Efficient time management is crucial, as students need to pace themselves to ensure they have sufficient time to address all questions in each module.

Covered Subjects

The Digital SAT® covers a comprehensive range of subjects to assess a student's readiness for college. The disciplines selected are carefully chosen to represent the competencies required for achievement in higher education.

Math

The Math section includes:

- *Algebra*: Focuses on linear equations, inequalities, and functions. Students must demonstrate an ability to solve equations, interpret linear functions, and understand algebraic expressions.
- *Geometry*: Covers the properties and applications of geometric shapes, including angles, circles, and triangles. Students frequently have to use geometric concepts to solve problems in order to resolve real-world issues.
- *Data Analysis*: Involves interpreting and analyzing data from tables, graphs, and charts. In order to make well-informed judgments based on evidence, students must comprehend probability and statistics.
- *Advanced Math*: Includes topics such as polynomial equations, exponents, and logarithms. This component assesses knowledge of mathematics beyond algebra and geometry at the intermediate level.

Reading & Writing

The Reading & Writing section encompasses:

- *Reading Comprehension*: Assesses the ability to understand and interpret written passages from various genres, including literature, science, and social studies. Students must identify main ideas, themes, and supporting details.
- *Evidence-Based Reading*: Requires students to find and use evidence from texts to support their answers. Analytical writing and critical thinking both require this ability.
- *Writing and Language*: Tests grammar, punctuation, and the effective use of language. Students must revise and edit texts to improve clarity, coherence, and correctness.
- *Integration of Knowledge and Ideas*: Involves synthesizing information from multiple sources and understanding how different texts relate to each other.

Permitted Tools

The Digital SAT® allows the use of specific tools to aid students during the exam. These tools are integrated into the digital testing platform and are designed to assist without giving an unfair advantage.

- **Calculator**: For the Math part, students can use the testing platform's built-in digital calculator. This calculator is available for all problems in the Math portion, demonstrating the test's emphasis on problem-solving abilities over manual computation. The calculator has both basic and advanced functions for solving more difficult issues.
- **Scratch Paper**: Students are given scratch paper to solve issues and take notes. This is especially important in the Math portion, where students may need to complete intermediate procedures or visualize geometric shapes.

Highlighting and Annotation Tools

The digital testing platform provides tools for highlighting text and creating annotations. These tools are useful in the Reading & Writing part because they allow students to highlight relevant passages and jot down quick notes to help them comprehend and analyze.

Review and Flagging

Within each module, students can flag questions for review, which enables them to bypass challenging topics and come back to them at a later time, if time permits. This tool aids in time management and guarantees that students do not spend too long on a single question.

Understanding the structure and features of the Digital SAT® is critical for successful preparation. Students can improve their performance by being familiar with the exam's adaptive format, time limitations, covered subjects, and permissible resources. As we proceed through this book, we will delve further into each topic area, providing thorough analysis, practice questions, and expert advice to help students earn the highest possible score on the Digital SAT®.

QUESTION BREAKDOWN AND SCORING METHODOLOGY

Understanding the question breakdown and scoring mechanism of the Digital SAT® is critical for students aiming for a high score. This section gives a detailed examination of the exam's question categories, distribution across sections, and scoring procedures.

The scoring process of the Digital SAT® is intended to provide a precise assessment of a student's ability. To calculate a final score, the ratings from each component are tallied independently.

Because the Digital SAT® uses an adaptive testing methodology, a student's performance in the first module determines how difficult the questions are in the second module. Here's how this impacts scoring:

- **Initial Performance Assessment**: In the first module, students encounter questions of varying difficulty. The second module's questions are harder or easier depending on how well they succeed on these.
- **Adaptive Module**: More difficult problems will be found in the second module if a student does well in the first. Conversely, if a student struggles in the first module, the second module will present easier questions.
- **Scoring Ranges**: Each question has a specific weight based on its difficulty. Correct answers to more difficult questions contribute more to the final score than correct answers to easier questions.

Raw Scores and Scaled Scores

In order to score an exam, raw scores—the total number of right answers—must be converted into scaled scores, which are the results that universities get.

- **Raw Score Calculation**: The raw score is increased by one point for each right response. You should try answering every question because there is no penalty for giving the wrong response.
- **Scaling Process**: Equating is a procedure that converts raw ratings to scaled scores. This guarantees score comparability between different exam formats and administrations. For both the reading and writing and math sections, the scaled score runs from 200 to 800, giving a total score between 400 and 1600.

Subscores and Cross-Test Scores

In addition to the main section scores, the Digital SAT® provides subscores and cross-test scores that offer a more detailed analysis of a student's performance.

- **Subscores**: These are provided for specific skill areas within each section, such as Command of Evidence, Words in Context, Heart of Algebra, Problem Solving and Data Analysis, and Passport to Advanced Math.
- **Cross-Test Scores**: The performance on questions measuring skills in Science and Analysis in History/Social Studies, which integrate skills across several disciplines, is reflected in these scores.

Practical Implications for Students

Understanding the question breakdown and scoring methodology allows students to develop effective test-taking strategies. Here are some practical tips:

1. **Prioritize High-Weight Questions**: Focus on answering more difficult questions correctly, as they contribute more to the final score.
2. **Maximize Raw Scores**: Since there is no penalty for giving the wrong response, try answering every question. Anything is preferable to a blank inquiry, even a hunch.
3. **Use Practice Tests Wisely**: Take lengthy practice exams under timed conditions to become acquainted with the structure and format of the test's questions.
4. **Focus on Weak Areas**: Use subscores to identify and improve on weaker areas, ensuring a balanced performance across all sections.

By mastering the question types and knowing how your performance affects your ultimate score, you may take the Digital SAT® with confidence and a strategic mentality. This knowledge not only helps you maximize your score, but it also lessens tension by explaining the exam process.

CHAPTER 2: SAT® MATH - BASIC MATHEMATICS

FUNDAMENTAL ALGEBRA AND ARITHMETIC

Fundamental Algebra and Arithmetic are the foundation of the SAT® Math portion, requiring not only a good understanding of basic ideas but also the ability to apply these concepts in a variety of circumstances. This chapter seeks to provide students with a broad understanding of these core areas, preparing them to tackle the variety of problems provided on the Digital SAT®.

The SAT®'s algebra focuses on manipulating expressions, solving equations, and interpreting functions. These ideas, which are heavily represented on the test, are essential to higher-level mathematics.

Linear Equations and Inequalities

Linear equations are algebraic expressions that equate to a straight line when graphed. They typically appear in the form $(ax + b = c)$, where (a), (b), and (c) are constants. Solving these equations involves isolating the variable (x):

$$ax + b = c$$

Subtract (b) from both sides:
$$ax = c - b$$

Divide by (a):

$$x = \frac{c-b}{a}$$

For example, to solve $(3x + 4 = 19)$:
$$3x + 4 = 19$$

Subtract 4:
$$3x = 15$$

Divide by 3:
$$x = 5$$

Inequalities, such as $(2x - 5 < 7)$, follow similar steps but result in a range of values. Solving the inequality:
$$2x - 5 < 7$$

Add 5:
$$2x < 12$$

Divide by 2:
$$x < 6$$

The solution set $(x < 6)$ can be represented graphically on a number line.

Systems of Linear Equations

The goal of systems of equations is to determine the values of variables that concurrently fulfill several equations. Numerous techniques, such as substitution and elimination, can be used to solve these systems.

For instance, consider the system:
2x + y = 10
x - y = 1

Using substitution:
Solve the second equation for (x):
x = y + 1

Substitute (x) into the first equation:
2(y + 1) + y = 10
2y + 2 + y = 10
3y + 2 = 10
3y = 8
y = 8/3

Substitute (y) back into (x = y + 1):
$$x = \frac{8}{3} + 1$$
$$x = \frac{11}{3}$$

Thus, the solution is $x = \frac{11}{3}$ and $y = \frac{8}{3}$.

Quadratic Equations

Quadratic equations appear in the form $ax^2 + bx + c = 0$. They can be solved using factoring, completing the square, or the quadratic formula:

$$x = \frac{-b \pm \sqrt{b^2 - 4ac}}{2a}$$

Consider the equation $x^2 - 5x + 6 = 0$. Factoring yields:
(x - 2)(x - 3) = 0

Setting each factor to zero gives the solutions:
x - 2 = 0 implies x = 2
x - 3 = 0 implies x = 3

Functions

Understanding functions is crucial for the SAT®. Every input x that a function f(x) maps to a single output f(x) exists. Particularly significant are linear functions, such as f(x) = mx + b, where m represents the slope and b the y-intercept.
For example, the function f(x) = 2x + 3 describes a line with a slope of 2 and a y-intercept of 3. To find f(4):
f(4) = 2(4) + 3 = 8 + 3 = 11

Core Concepts in Arithmetic

Arithmetic on the SAT® encompasses fundamental operations, number properties, and proportional reasoning.

Basic Operations and Properties

Mastery of basic operations—addition, subtraction, division and multiplication —is essential. Understanding properties of numbers, such as commutative, associative, and distributive properties, can simplify complex calculations.
For example, using the distributive property to simplify 3(2 + 4):

$$3(2 + 4) = 3 \cdot 2 + 3 \cdot 4 = 6 + 12 = 18$$

Fractions and Decimals

Competence with fractions and decimals is crucial. This includes operations with fractions, such as addition, subtraction, division and multiplication.

To add fractions, find a common denominator:

$$\frac{2}{5} + \frac{3}{4}$$

The least common denominator is 20:

$$\frac{2 \cdot 4}{5 \cdot 4} + \frac{3 \cdot 5}{4 \cdot 5} = \frac{8}{20} + \frac{15}{20} = \frac{23}{20} = 1\frac{3}{20}$$

Ratios and Proportions

Understanding ratios and proportions is vital for solving many real-world problems. In contrast to a proportion, which asserts that two ratios are equal, a ratio compares two quantities.

For instance, if the ratio of students to teachers is 4:1 and there are 120 students, the number of teachers is found by setting up a proportion:

$4/1 = 120/x$

Solving for x:

$4x = 120$

$x = 120/4$

$x = 30$

Percentages

Percentages are a common topic, involving calculations of parts per hundred. To find 20% of 50:

$0.20 \times 50 = 10$

For percentage change, use the formula:

$$\textbf{Percentage Change} = \left(\frac{\text{New Value} - \text{Old Value}}{\text{Old Value}}\right) \times 100\%$$

If a price increases from $40 to $50:

$$\textbf{Percentage Change} = \left(\frac{50 - 40}{40}\right) \times 100\% = \frac{10}{40} \times 100\% = 25\%$$

These fundamental algebraic and arithmetic principles are not only theoretical; they have practical applications. Understanding linear equations and inequalities is important for budgeting, whereas ratios and proportions are important in industries such as cuisine, architecture, and engineering.

Students who understand these fundamental areas can approach the SAT® Math part with confidence, knowing they have the abilities to solve a variety of problems effectively. The ability to manipulate equations, interpret functions, and perform fundamental arithmetic operations serves as the foundation for advanced mathematical thinking and problem solving, which are required not only for the SAT® but also for future academic and professional success.

BASIC GEOMETRY

Geometry is an important part of the SAT® Math section because it tests students' comprehension of shapes, sizes, figure relative locations, and spatial features. Mastering basic geometry concepts is critical for success on the Digital SAT® because it lays the groundwork for more complicated mathematical reasoning necessary in further education and numerous professions.

Fundamentally, geometry is the study of the characteristics and connections of surfaces, solids, lines, and points. The SAT® emphasizes practical applications of these ideas, asking students to answer questions involving angles, triangles, circles, and other polygons.

Points, Lines, and Angles

Learning the fundamentals of points, lines, and angles is critical. A point indicates a position in space, but a line is a one-dimensional figure that extends indefinitely in both directions. An angle is generated by two rays (angle sides) that have a common terminal (the vertex).

Types of Angles
- *Acute Angle*: Less than 90 degrees.
- *Right Angle*: Exactly 90 degrees.
- *Obtuse Angle*: Between 90 and 180 degrees.
- *Straight Angle*: Exactly 180 degrees.

Calculating the sum of angles is often required. For instance, the inner angles of a triangle always add up to 180 degrees. Consider a problem where one angle of a triangle is 90 degrees (right triangle), and another angle is 45 degrees. To find the third angle:

Sum of angles in a triangle = 180°

$90° + 45° +$ Third angle $= 180°$

Third angle $= 180° - 135°$

Third angle $= 45°$

Triangles

Triangles are fundamental shapes in geometry, and understanding their properties is essential. Their sides and angles determine their classification.

Types of Triangles
- *Equilateral Triangle*: All sides and angles are equal. Each angle is 60 degrees.
- *Isosceles Triangle*: Has two equal sides and two equal angles.
- *Scalene Triangle*: All sides and angles are different.
- *Right Triangle*: One angle is 90 degrees.

The Pythagorean theorem is a critical concept in right triangles:

$a^2 + b^2 = c^2$

Where a and b are the legs of the triangle, and c is the hypotenuse. For example, in a right triangle with legs of 3 and 4 units:

$3^2 + 4^2 = c^2$

$9 + 16 = c^2$

$25 = c^2$

$c = 5$

Understanding special right triangles, such as the 45-45-90 and 30-60-90 triangles, also aids in solving SAT® problems more efficiently.

- **45-45-90 Triangle**: The hypotenuse is equal to twice the length of a leg, and the legs are congruent.
- **30-60-90 Triangle**: The length of the hypotenuse is twice the length of the shorter leg, and the length of the longer leg is square root of 3 times the length of the shorter leg.

Quadrilaterals and Polygons

Quadrilaterals, such as squares, rectangles, and parallelograms, are also common on the SAT®. Every one of them has unique qualities that can be applied to solve issues.

- **Square**: All sides and angles are equal. The area is s^2, where s is the length of a side.
- **Rectangle**: Every angle is 90 degrees, and there are equal opposite sides. The area is expressed as l x w, where w denotes width and l equals length.
- **Parallelogram**: Opposite sides are parallel and equal. The area is b x h, where b is the base and h is the height.

Polygons with more than four sides also appear on the SAT®, and understanding their properties is essential.

- **Regular Polygon**: All sides and angles are equal. The sum of the interior angles of an n-sided polygon is (n-2) x 180°.

For example, a regular hexagon (6-sided polygon) has interior angles summing to:
(6-2) x 180° = 720°

Each interior angle in a regular hexagon is:
720°/6 = 120°

Circles

Circles are another vital topic in geometry. Key concepts include the radius, diameter, circumference, and area.

- *Radius (r)*: Distance from the center to any point on the circle.
- *Diameter (d)*: Twice the radius, d = 2r.
- *Circumference (C)*: Distance around the circle, C = 2 πr or πd.
- *Area (A)*: Space enclosed by the circle, $A = \pi r^2$.

Consider a circle with a radius of 3 units. The circumference and area are calculated as follows:
C = 2π x 3 = 6π
A = π x 3² = 9π

Coordinate Geometry

Coordinate geometry combines algebra and geometry, allowing for the graphical representation of geometric figures and the solution of geometric problems using algebraic equations.

- *Distance Formula*: To find the distance between two points (x_1, y_1) and (x_2, y_2):

$$\text{Distance} = \sqrt{(x_2 - x_1)^2 + (y_2 - y_1)^2}$$

For points (1, 2) and (4, 6):

$$\text{Distance} = \sqrt{(4 - 1)^2 + (6 - 2)^2} = \sqrt{3^2 + 4^2} = \sqrt{9 + 16} = \sqrt{25} = 5$$

- *Midpoint Formula*: To find the midpoint of a line segment between points (x_1, y_1) and (x_2, y_2):

$$\text{Midpoint} = \left(\frac{x_1 + x_2}{2}, \frac{y_1 + y_2}{2} \right)$$

For points (1, 2) and (4, 6):

$$\text{Midpoint} = \left(\frac{1+4}{2}, \frac{2+6}{2}\right) = \left(\frac{5}{2}, \frac{8}{2}\right) = (2.5, 4)$$

- *Equation of a Line*: The slope-intercept form of a line is $y = mx + b$, where m is the slope and b is the y-intercept.

For a line passing through (1, 2) with a slope of 3:
$y - 2 = 3(x - 1)$

Solving for y:
$y - 2 = 3x - 3$
$y = 3x - 1$

Understanding geometric principles isn't just about solving textbook problems. Geometry has practical applications in engineering, architecture, and physics. For instance, architects employ geometric ideas to design structures that are both aesthetically pleasing and sound structurally. Engineers use geometry to build everything from circuits to mechanical systems, maximizing space and functionality.

CHAPTER 3: GRAPHS AND LINEAR EQUATIONS

SOLVING EQUATIONS

Algebra is built on equations, which are also necessary for resolving practical problems. Mastery of equation solving is vital for success on the Digital SAT® because it serves as the foundation for more complex mathematical topics. This chapter discusses the techniques and tactics used to solve various types of equations, with a focus on linear equations, systems of equations, and their applications.

Solving Equations with Variables on Both Sides
Sometimes, equations will have variables on both sides. To solve these, we must first get all the variable terms on one side and the constant terms on the other.
Example: Solve $2x + 3 = x - 4$.

1. Subtract x from both sides to get all x terms on one side:
$2x - x + 3 = x - x - 4$
$x + 3 = -4$

2. Subtract 3 from both sides to isolate x:
$x + 3 - 3 = -4 - 3$
$x = -7$

Linear Equations with Fractions
Linear equations can also include fractions, which require careful handling to clear the denominators.

Example: Solve $\frac{2x}{3} - \frac{1}{2} = \frac{3}{4}$.

1. Find the fractions' common denominator. The least common multiple of 3, 2, and 4 in this instance is 12.

2. Multiply every term by 12 to clear the denominators:
$$12\left(\frac{2x}{3}\right) - 12\left(\frac{1}{2}\right) = 12\left(\frac{3}{4}\right)$$
$$8x - 6 = 9$$

3. Solve the resulting equation:
$8x - 6 = 9$
$8x = 15$
$x = 15/8$
$x = 1.875$

Substitution Method
By solving one equation for a single variable and then replacing that expression into the other equation, one can employ the substitution approach.
Example: Solve the system
$y = 2x + 3$
$3x - y = 7$

1. Substitute $y = 2x + 3$ into the second equation:
$3x - (2x + 3) = 7$
$3x - 2x - 3 = 7$
$x - 3 = 7$

$x = 10$

2. Substitute $x = 10$ back into the first equation to find y:
$y = 2(10) + 3$
$y = 20 + 3$
$y = 23$

Thus, the solution is (10, 23).

Elimination Method

Equations are added or subtracted as part of the elimination procedure to remove one variable and allow the remaining variable to be solved for.

Example: Solve the system
$2x + 3y = 13$
$4x - 3y = 11$

1. Add the two equations to eliminate y:
$(2x + 3y) + (4x - 3y) = 13 + 11$
$6x = 24$
$x = 4$

2. Substitute $x = 4$ back into one of the original equations to find y:
$2(4) + 3y = 13$
$8 + 3y = 13$
$3y = 5$
$y = 5/3$

Thus, the solution is (4, 5/3).

WORD PROBLEMS AND APPLICATIONS

Word problems are an important component of the Digital SAT®, which assesses a student's ability to apply mathematical principles to real-world situations. These challenges necessitate not only mathematical aptitude, but also the capacity to interpret and convert verbal descriptions into mathematical formulae. This chapter looks at several types of word problems and offers solutions for dealing with them effectively.

The information presented must be transformed into a mathematical equation as the first step in solving a word problem. This entails identifying the unknowns, determining the information provided, and developing an equation that connects these aspects.

Example 1: Distance, Rate, and Time

Consider a problem where a student needs to calculate the time taken for a journey. Suppose a car travels at a constant speed of 60 miles per hour. What is the estimated time required to travel 150 miles?

1. Identify the variables:
- Distance (d): 150 miles
- Rate (r): 60 miles per hour
- Time (t): Unknown

2. Use the formula $d = rt$ to set up the equation:
$150 = 60t$

3. Solve for t:

$t = 150/60 = 2.5$

Thus, the journey will take 2.5 hours.

Example 2: Proportions and Ratios

Word problems involving proportions and ratios are common on the SAT®. These problems require understanding how different quantities relate to each other.

For every two cups of sugar in a recipe, three cups of flour are needed. If a baker wants to make a larger batch using 9 cups of flour, how much sugar is needed?

1. Identify the ratio and set up the proportion:

$$\frac{3 \text{ cups of flour}}{2 \text{ cups of sugar}} = \frac{9 \text{ cups of flour}}{x \text{ cups of sugar}}$$

2. Solve for x:

$3x = 18$

$x = 6$

Therefore, 6 cups of sugar are needed.

Example 3: Percentages

Percentage problems often involve finding parts of a whole or changes in quantities.

There is a sale going on which all merchandise is 25% off. How much is the jacket on sale for if its original cost was $80?

1. Identify the original price and the discount:
   - Original price (P): $80
   - Discount (D): 25%

2. Calculate the amount of the discount:

$D = 0.25 \times 80 = 20$

3. Subtract the discount from the original price:

Sale price $= 80 - 20 = 60$

The sale price of the jacket is $60.

Example 4: Systems of Equations

Some word problems involve systems of linear equations, requiring simultaneous solutions for multiple variables.

Two friends are saving money to buy a concert ticket. Together, they save $100. If one friend saves $10 more than twice what the other saves, how much does each friend save?

1. Let x represent the amount saved by the first friend and y the amount saved by the second friend.
2. Set up the system of equations:

$x + y = 100$

$x = 2y + 10$

3. Substitute x from the second equation into the first:

$2y + 10 + y = 100$

$3y + 10 = 100$

$3y = 90$

$y = 30$

4. Substitute y back into the second equation:
x = 2(30) + 10 = 70

Therefore, the first friend saves $70, and the second friend saves $30.

Strategies for Tackling Word Problems
Word issue solving demands a methodical approach to be successful. Here are some helpful strategies:
1. **Read Carefully**: Comprehend the issue and determine the pertinent details. Emphasize or underscore crucial information.
2. **Define Variables**: Give a clear explanation of what each variable means. To prevent confusion, use symbols that have significance.
3. **Formulate Equations**: Translate the word problem into one or more mathematical equations.
4. **Solve Systematically**: Use appropriate mathematical techniques to solve the equations. Check your work to ensure accuracy.
5. **Interpret the Solution**: Make sure the solution makes sense in the context of the problem. Verify units and other details.

Word problems and their applications are an important part of the SAT® Math exam, demanding both mathematical knowledge and practical problem-solving abilities. Students can dramatically enhance their Digital SAT® performance by knowing how to interpret real-world circumstances into mathematical equations and solve them in a systematic manner. With practice and mastery of these approaches, students can tackle word problems with confidence and accuracy, ensuring they are well-prepared for the exam's demands.

PLOTTING LINEAR EQUATIONS

Plotting linear equations is a crucial mathematical ability, particularly in algebra. This chapter will look at the physics of charting linear equations on a Cartesian plane, the importance of slopes and intercepts, and how to effectively visualize these equations.

A two-dimensional plane having a horizontal (x) and vertical (y) axis is known as the Cartesian plane, after the French mathematician René Descartes. The coordinates (0,0) denote the origin, which is the point where these axes intersect. On this plane, every point may be uniquely recognized by two numerical coordinates (x, y).

Linear Equations in Slope-Intercept Form
There are several ways to express a linear equation, but the slope-intercept form, which is provided by:

y = mx + b

In this equation:
- y represents the dependent variable.
- x represents the independent variable.
- m represents the slope of the line.
- b represents the y-intercept, which is the point where the line crosses the y-axis.

Understanding Slope and Intercept
A line's slope (m) indicates both its direction and steepness. It is calculated as the ratio of the change in y (rise) to the change in x (run):

$$m = \frac{\Delta y}{\Delta x} = \frac{y_2 - y_1}{x_2 - x_1}$$

The y-intercept b is the value of y when x is zero. It shows the location of the line's y-axis crossing.

Plotting a Linear Equation

To plot a linear equation, follow these steps:

1. *Identify the Slope and Y-Intercept*: For the equation $y = 2x + 3$, the slope m is 2, and the y-intercept b is 3.

2. *Plot the Y-Intercept*: Begin by plotting the y-intercept on the Cartesian plane. In this case, mark the point (0, 3).

3. *Use the Slope to Find Another Point*: Starting from the y-intercept, use the slope to determine another point on the line. Since the slope is 2, it means that for every 1 unit increase in x, y increases by 2 units. From (0, 3), move right 1 unit to (1, 5).

4. *Draw the Line*: Draw a line that extends in both directions from the spots.

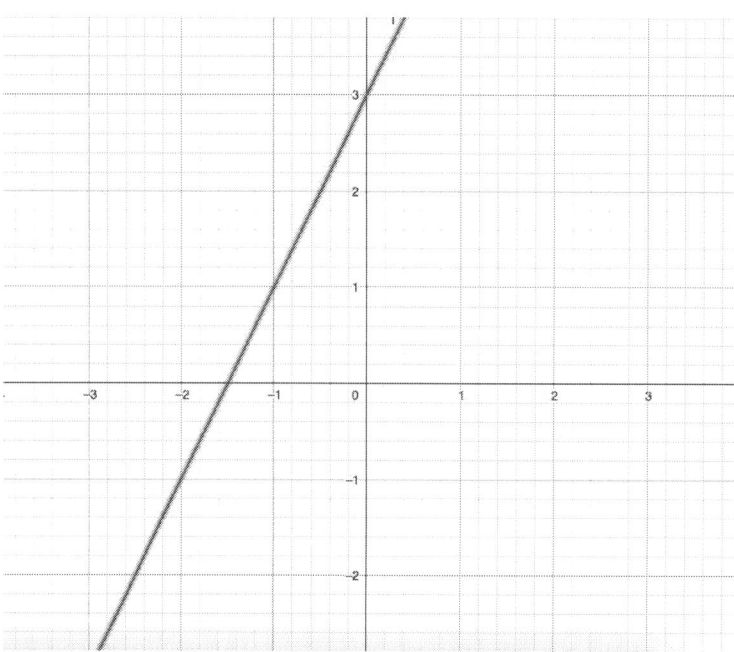

Examples and Practice

Let's explore additional examples to solidify the concept.

Example 1: Plotting $y = -(1/2)x + 4$

1. Identify the Slope and Y-Intercept: The slope is $-(1/2)$, and the y-intercept is 4.

2. Plot the Y-Intercept: Mark the point (0, 4).

3. Use the Slope to Find Another Point: From (0, 4), move right 2 units (since Delta x = 2) and down 1 unit (since Delta y = -1) to (2, 3).

4. Draw the Line: Connect the points (0, 4) and (2, 3).

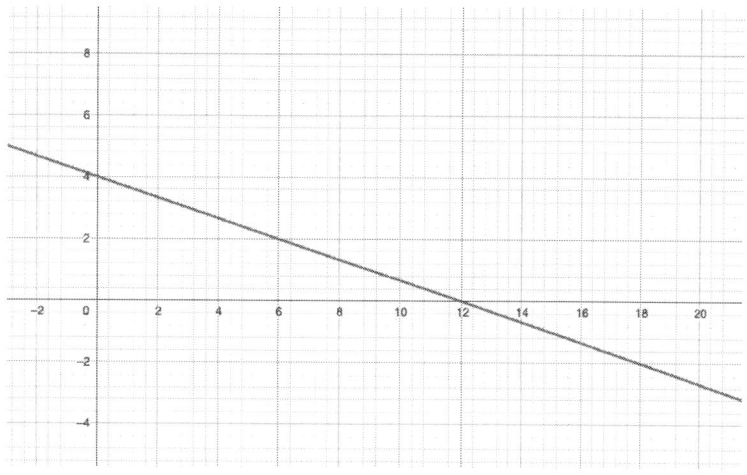

Example 2: Plotting y = 3

This equation is a horizontal line where y is always 3, regardless of x.

1. Identify the Y-Intercept: The y-intercept is 3.
2. Plot Points: Mark points such as (0, 3), (1, 3), and (-1, 3).
3. Draw the Line: Use a straight line that is parallel to the x-axis to connect these spots.

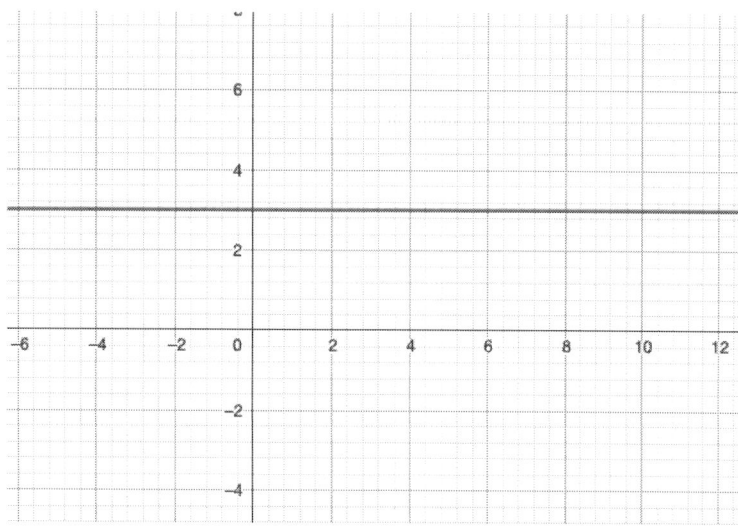

Special Cases: Vertical Lines

Vertical lines are represented by equations of the form x = a, where a is the x-intercept. These lines have an undefined slope.

Example: Plotting x = -2

1. Identify the X-Intercept: The x-intercept is -2.
2. Plot Points: Mark points such as (-2, 0), (-2, 1), and (-2, -1).
3. Draw the Line: Connect these points with a straight line parallel to the y-axis.

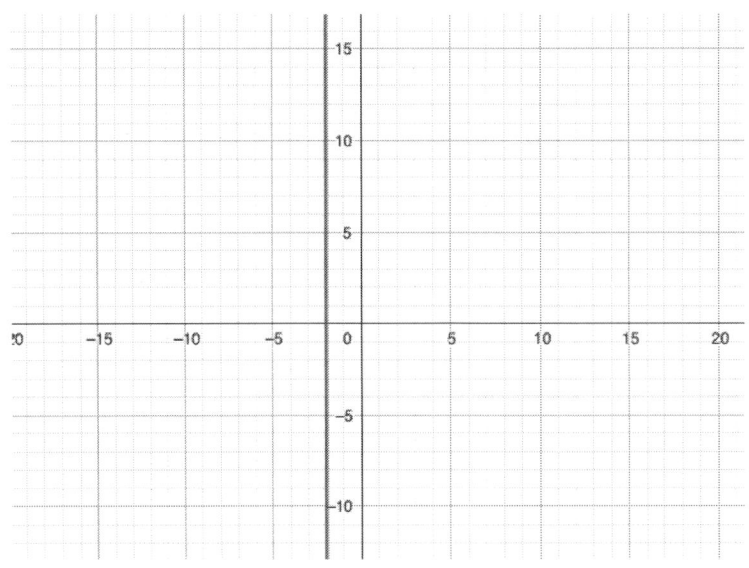

Converting Equations to Slope-Intercept Form

Slope-intercept form is not always used to represent linear equations. Sometimes, it's necessary to rearrange the equation.

Example: Converting 2x - 3y = 6 to Slope-Intercept Form
1. Isolate y:
2x - 3y = 6
-3y = -2x + 6
y = (2/3) x - 2

Now the equation is in slope-intercept form, with a slope of 2/3 and a y-intercept of -2.

Plotting the Converted Equation
1. Identify the Slope and Y-Intercept: The slope is 2/3 and the y-intercept is -2.
2. Plot the Y-Intercept: Mark the point (0, -2).
3. Use the Slope to Find Another Point: From (0, -2), move right 3 units and up 2 units to (3, 0).
4. Draw the Line: Connect the points (0, -2) and (3, 0).

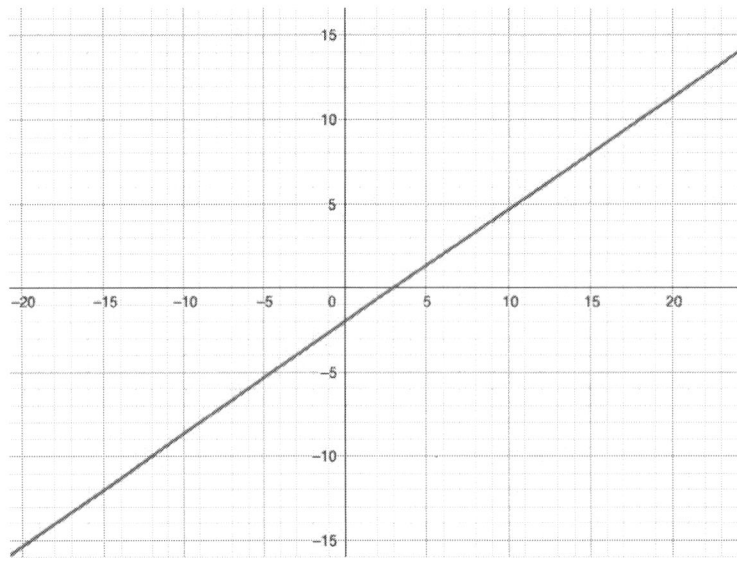

20

CHAPTER 4: SYSTEMS OF LINEAR EQUATIONS

COMBINATION METHOD

An efficient algebraic strategy for resolving systems of linear equations is the Combination Method, sometimes referred to as the Addition Method or the Elimination Method. This method involves solving for the remaining variable by adding or subtracting equations to get rid of one of the variables. Understanding and mastering this method is critical for success on the Digital SAT®, as it arises frequently in a variety of problem-solving scenarios.

The Combination Method is very beneficial for dealing with linear equation systems in which one of the variables' coefficients is either equal or opposite. One variable is eliminated by carefully adding or subtracting these equations, leaving the system with just one equation and one unknown.

Consider the following system of equations:

$3x + 2y = 16$

$5x - 2y = 4$

By adding these equations, the y terms cancel out:

$(3x + 2y) + (5x - 2y) = 16 + 4$

$8x = 20$

$x = 20/8$

$x = 2.5$

To find y, put the determined value of x back into one of the original equations:

$3(2.5) + 2y = 16$

$7.5 + 2y = 16$

$2y = 16 - 7.5$

$2y = 8.5$

$y = 8.5/2$

$y = 4.25$

Thus, the solution to the system is $x = 2.5$ and $y = 4.25$.

Step-by-Step Process

To effectively use the Combination Method, follow these steps:

1. **Align Equations**: Write the equations in standard form $ax + by = c$.
2. **Equalize Coefficients**: In order to have the opposites of one variable's coefficients, adjust the equations.
3. **Add or Subtract Equations**: Integrate the formulas to remove one variable.
4. **Solve for the Remaining Variable**: Solve the resulting equation.
5. **Substitute Back**: To determine the other variable, rewrite one of the original equations using the discovered value.

Example 1: Simple Elimination

Solve the system:

$4x + 6y = 24$

$2x - 6y = 6$

1. Align Equations: Already aligned.
2. Equalize Coefficients: The coefficients of y are already opposites.
3. Add Equations:

$(4x + 6y) + (2x - 6y) = 24 + 6$

$6x = 30$

$x = 30/6$

x = 5

4. Substitute Back: Substitute x = 5 into the second equation:
2(5) - 6y = 6
10 - 6y = 6
-6y = -4
y = (-4)/(-6)
y = 2/3

Thus, the solution is x = 5 and y = 2/3

Example 2: Scaling Equations
Sometimes, it is necessary to scale equations to equalize coefficients.
Solve the system:
3x + 4y = 20
5x + 2y = 14

1.Align Equations: Already aligned.
2. Equalize Coefficients: Multiply the first equation by 2 and the second by 4 to make the coefficients of y equal:
2(3x + 4y) = 2(20)
6x + 8y = 40
4(5x + 2y) = 4(14)
20x + 8y = 56

3. Subtract Equations:
(20x + 8y) - (6x + 8y) = 56 - 40
14x = 16
x = 16/14
x = 8/7

4. Substitute Back: Substitute x = 8/7 into the first equation:

$$3 \left(\tfrac{8}{7} \right) + 4y = 20$$
$$\tfrac{24}{7} + 4y = 20$$
$$4y = 20 - \tfrac{24}{7}$$
$$4y = \tfrac{140-24}{7}$$
$$4y = \tfrac{116}{7}$$
$$y = \tfrac{116}{28}$$
$$y = \tfrac{29}{7}$$

Thus, the solution is x = 8/7 and y = 29/7

Applications and Practical Problems
The Combination Method is not confined to algebraic issues; it has several applications in economics, engineering, and the sciences. Understanding how to apply this strategy to real-world challenges makes it more useful and relevant.

Example: Economic Planning
A company produces two products, A and B. The total production cost for A and B together is $5,000, and producing one unit of A costs twice as much as producing one unit of B. If the total number of units produced is 150, determine the cost

of producing one unit of each product.

1. Let x be the cost of producing one unit of A and y be the cost of producing one unit of B.
2. Set up the system of equations based on the given information:

$x + y = 5000$

$x = 2y$

3. Substitute $x = 2y$ into the first equation:

$2y + y = 5000$

$3y = 5000$

$y = 5000/3$

$y = 1666.67$

4. Substitute y back into the second equation:

$x = 2(1666.67)$

$x = 3333.34$

Thus, the cost of producing one unit of product A is $3333.34, and one unit of product B is $1666.67.

Example: Engineering
In an engineering context, consider a problem involving two materials with different properties. Suppose you need to mix two solutions, one with 40% concentration and another with 60% concentration, to obtain 100 liters of a 50% solution. For each solution, how many liters are needed?

1. Let x represent the 40% solution's liters and y represent the 60% solution's liters.
2. Set up the system of equations:

$x + y = 100$

$0.4x + 0.6y = 0.5 \times 100$

3. Simplify the second equation:

$0.4x + 0.6y = 50$

$4x + 6y = 500$

$2x + 3y = 250$

4. Multiply the first equation by 2:

$2x + 2y = 200$

5. Subtract the first equation from the second:

$(2x + 3y) - (2x + 2y) = 250 - 200$

$y = 50$

6. Substitute $y = 50$ back into the first equation:

$x + 50 = 100$

$x = 50$

Thus, 50 liters of the 40% solution and 50 liters of the 60% solution are required.

Students can use the Combination Method to efficiently solve systems of linear equations, improving their problem-solving skills for the Digital SAT® and beyond. Mastering this technique lays a solid basis for tackling challenging mathematical problems and real-world applications.

DETERMINING THE NUMBER OF SOLUTIONS

When studying a system of linear equations, it is essential to comprehend how many alternative solutions there are. This information aids in assessing the nature of the system and choosing the best approaches for solving it. There may be one solution, an infinite number of solutions, or no solutions at all for a system of linear equations. The criteria and procedures used to determine how many solutions there are to a given system of linear equations are covered in this chapter. Combining two or more linear equations with the same set of variables results in a system of linear equations. A set of variable values satisfying each equation simultaneously is the system's solution. A system of two linear equations in two variables is represented geometrically by a pair of planar lines.

Unique Solution
When a system of linear equations represents lines that intersect at a single location, the equations have a unique solution. This scenario occurs when the lines have different slopes, making them neither parallel nor identical.

Consider the system:

2x + 3y = 6

x - 2y = 1

To determine the number of solutions, we can graph the equations or use algebraic methods such as substitution or elimination. After algebraically solving the system, we arrive at:

1. To align the coefficients of x, multiply the second equation by two:

2(x - 2y) = 2(1)

2x - 4y = 2

2. Subtract the second equation from the first:

(2x + 3y) - (2x - 4y) = 6 - 2

7y = 4

y = 4/7

3. Substitute y back into the first equation:

$$2x + 3\left(\frac{4}{7}\right) = 6$$

$$2x + \frac{12}{7} = 6$$

$$2x = 6 - \frac{12}{7}$$

$$2x = \frac{42}{7} - \frac{12}{7}$$

$$2x = \frac{30}{7}$$

$$x = \frac{15}{7}$$

Thus, the solution is (15/7, 4/7), indicating a unique solution.

Infinitely Many Solutions
When the equations represent the same line, which is known as coincident lines, then a system has an infinite number of solutions. This scenario occurs when the equations are proportional to each other.

Consider the system:

2x + 4y = 8

x + 2y = 4

To determine the number of solutions, we can manipulate one equation to see if it matches the other:

1. Multiply the second equation by 2:

$2(x + 2y) = 2(4)$

$2x + 4y = 8$

Since the equations are identical, they represent the same line. There are an endless number of options because each point on this line represents a potential solution.

No Solution

When the equations indicate parallel lines that do not intersect, the system is solved. This situation arises when the lines have distinct y-intercepts but the same slope.

Consider the system:

$3x - 2y = 6$

$3x - 2y = 12$

To determine the number of solutions, we can compare the equations:

1. Subtract the first equation from the second:

$(3x - 2y) - (3x - 2y) = 12 - 6$

$0 = 6$

There cannot be a solution because this contradiction shows that the lines are parallel and do not overlap.

Analyzing the Coefficients

To determine the number of solutions algebraically, we can analyze the coefficients of the equations. Consider a system of two equations in the form:

$a_1x + b_1y = c_1$

$a_2x + b_2y = c_2$

1. *Unique Solution*: The system has a unique solution if the ratio of the coefficients of x and y are not equal:

$$\frac{a_1}{a_2} \neq \frac{b_1}{b_2}$$

2. *Infinitely Many Solutions*: If the constant ratio and the coefficient ratios of x and y are both identical, then there are an endless number of solutions to the system:

$$\frac{a_1}{a_2} = \frac{b_1}{b_2} = \frac{c_1}{c_2}$$

3. *No Solution*: If the coefficient ratios of x and y are identical, but the constant ratio is not, the system cannot be solved:

$$\frac{a_1}{a_2} = \frac{b_1}{b_2} \neq \frac{c_1}{c_2}$$

Example: Analyzing Coefficients

Consider the system:

$4x + 6y = 8$

$2x + 3y = 4$

1. Calculate the ratios:

$4/2 = 2$

$6/3 = 2$

$8/4 = 2$

Since the ratios are equal, the system has infinitely many solutions.

Graphical Interpretation

Graphical representation helps visualize the number of solutions. Plotting the equations on the Cartesian plane can confirm the nature of the solutions:

1. **Unique Solution**: Lines intersect at one point.
2. **Infinitely Many Solutions**: Lines coincide.
3. **No Solution**: Lines are parallel and distinct.

Example: Graphical Analysis

Consider the system:

$y = 2x + 1$
$y = 2x + 4$

Plotting these equations:

1. The first equation $y = 2x + 1$ has a slope of 2 and a y-intercept of 1.
2. The second equation $y = 2x + 4$ has a slope of 2 and a y-intercept of 4.

The lines are parallel and do not intersect, indicating no solution.

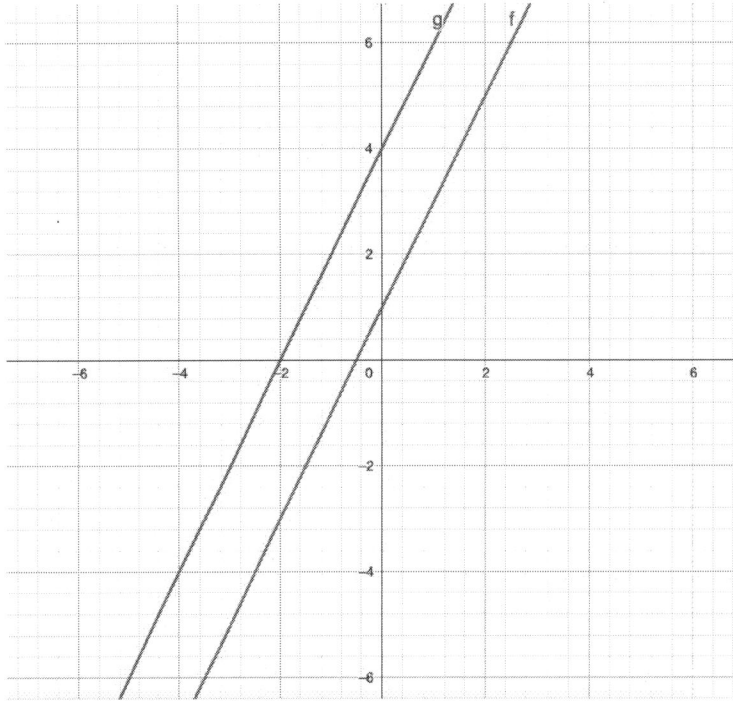

Example: Engineering Application

An engineer is designing a truss structure where the forces in the members must satisfy a system of linear equations. Finding the number of solutions contributes to the stability and statically determinateness of the structure.

Consider the system representing the forces:

$F_1 + F_2 = 100$
$2F_1 + 3F_2 = 250$

Analyze the coefficients:

$$\frac{1}{2} \neq \frac{1}{3}$$

The ratios are not equal, indicating a unique solution, ensuring the truss is statically determinate.

Example: Economic Application

In an economic model, a company analyzes the cost and revenue functions to determine the break-even point. The total cost and entire revenue are represented by the system of equations.

Consider the system:

$C = 50x + 200$

$R = 70x$

Where C is the total cost, R is the total revenue, and x is the number of units produced and sold.

To find the break-even point, set $C = R$:

$50x + 200 = 70x$

$200 = 20x$

$x = 10$

The unique solution $x = 10$ indicates the company must produce and sell 10 units to break even.

Students can improve their problem-solving and analytical skills by learning how to calculate the number of solutions to systems of linear equations. This knowledge is required for success on the Digital SAT® and serves as a solid foundation for future study in mathematics and its applications in a variety of fields.

CHAPTER 5: INEQUALITIES

SOLVING LINEAR INEQUALITIES

A fundamental component of algebra, linear inequalities are essential to many mathematical and practical applications. Students getting ready for the Digital SAT® need to know how to solve these inequalities and graphically portray their answers. With thorough explanations and useful examples, this chapter offers a thorough investigation of solving linear inequalities.

Similar to linear equations, linear inequalities also use inequality symbols (\, ≤, >, ≥) in place of the equal sign. Rather of defining a single solution, these inequalities define a range of feasible values for the variables involved.

Consider the inequality:

$3x + 2 < 11$

This inequality states that $3x + 2$ must be less than 11. Once the variable on one side of the inequality is isolated, we can solve for x.

Step-by-Step Process for Solving Linear Inequalities
1. **Isolate the Variable**: To determine which variable is on one side of the inequality, apply algebraic procedures.
2. **Simplify the Inequality**: Perform any necessary simplification to make the inequality easier to solve.
3. **Flip the Inequality Sign When Multiplying or Dividing by a Negative Number**: In case you divide or multiply both sides by a negative value, don't forget to flip the inequality sign.
4. **Express the Solution**: Use interval notation or a number line to graphically depict the solution.

Example 1: Solving a Simple Inequality
Solve the inequality:

$3x + 2 < 11$

1. Subtract 2 from both sides:
$3x < 9$
2. Divide both sides by 3:
$x < 3$

The solution is $x < 3$. All values smaller than three can be shown as this on a number line.

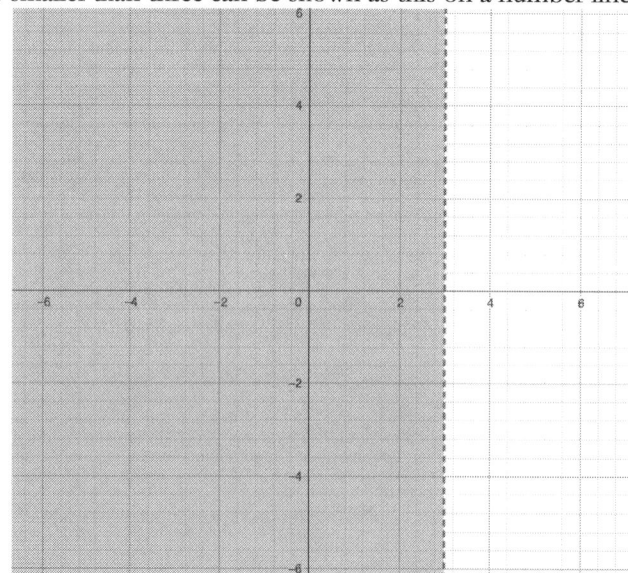

Example 2: Solving an Inequality with a Negative Coefficient

Solve the inequality:

$$-4x + 5 \geq 1$$

1. Subtract 5 from both sides:

$$-4x \geq -4$$

2. Remember to reverse the inequality sign and divide both sides by -4:

$$x \leq 1$$

The solution is x ≤ 1. All values that are less than or equal to one can be shown as this on a number line.

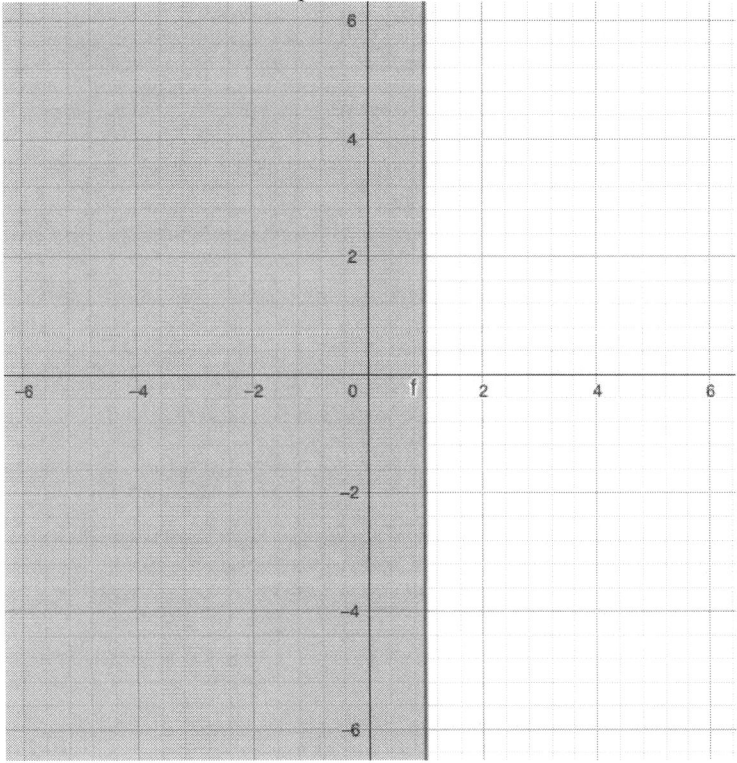

Compound Inequalities

Two distinct inequality united into a single sentence is known as a compound inequality. They can be written in two forms: "and" and "or".

Example 3: Solving a Compound Inequality ("And"*

Solve the compound inequality:

$$1 < 2x + 3 \leq 7$$

1. Divide the compound inequality into the following two distinct inequality:

$$1 < 2x + 3$$
$$2x + 3 \leq 7$$

2. Solve each inequality separately:

- For $1 < 2x + 3$:

$$1 - 3 < 2x$$
$$-2 < 2x$$
$$-1 < x$$
$$x > -1$$

- For $2x + 3 \leq 7$:

$$2x \leq 4$$
$$x \leq 2$$

3. Combine the solutions:

$$-1 < x \leq 2$$

The solution is $-1 < x \leq 2$. A number line with values from -1 to 2, inclusive, can be used to illustrate this.

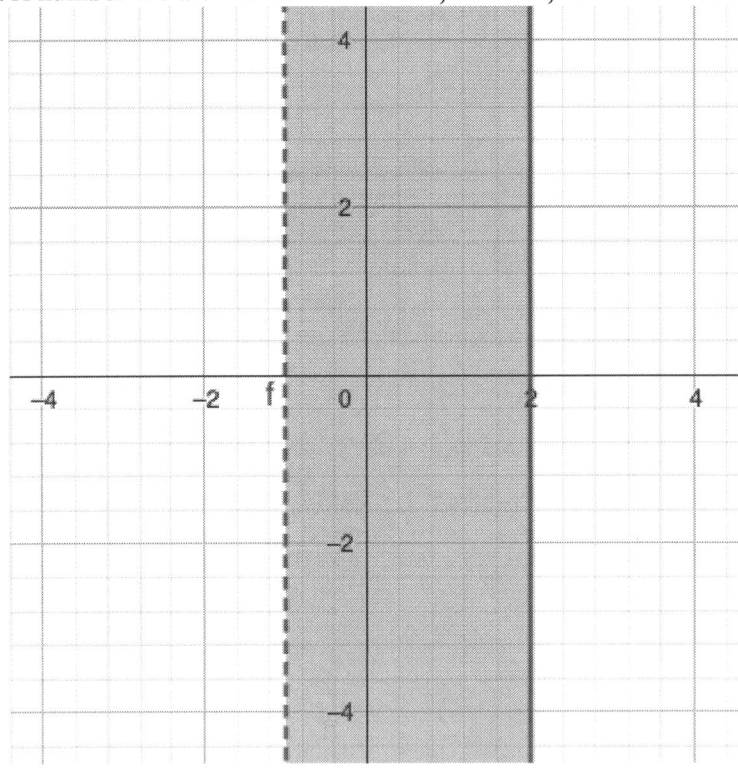

Example 4: Solving a Compound Inequality ("Or")
Solve the compound inequality:
2x - 1 < -3 or 3x + 2 > 11

1. Solve each inequality separately:

- For $2x - 1 < -3$:

  $2x < -2$

  $x < -1$

- For $3x + 2 > 11$:

  $3x > 9$

  $x > 3$

2. Combine the solutions:
x < -1 or x > 3

The solution is x < -1 or x > 3. A number line with values less than -1 or larger than 3 can be used to illustrate this.

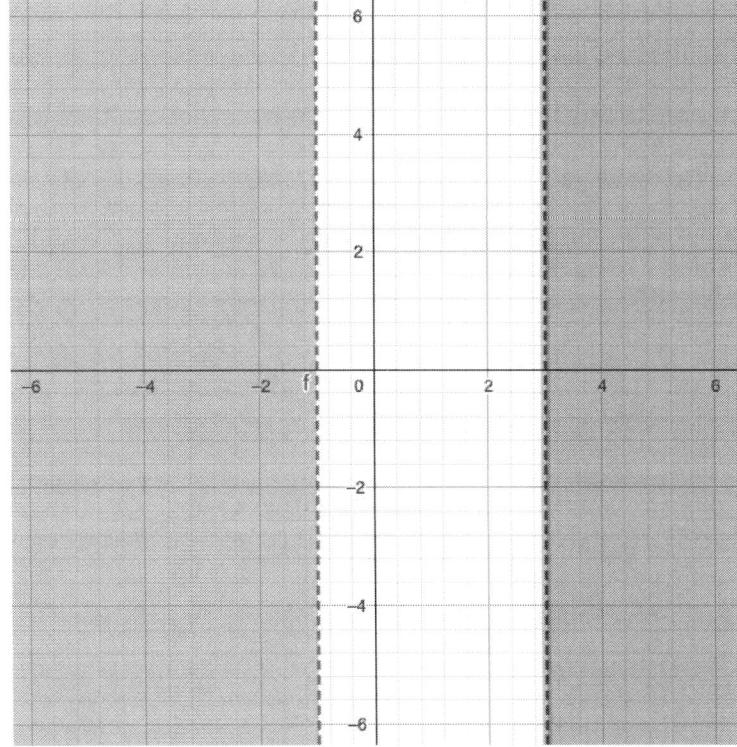

Students can enhance their problem-solving abilities and get a deeper comprehension of mathematical ideas by becoming proficient in the procedures for solving and graphing linear inequalities. These abilities have many uses in a variety of academic and professional domains, in addition to being essential for the Digital SAT®.

ANALYZING SYSTEM OF INEQUALITIES

Determining the feasible zone where all criteria are satisfied simultaneously and comprehending the interactions between numerous inequalities are key components of system analysis. When tackling real-world issues involving optimization and constraint satisfaction, this procedure is crucial. We will examine methods for graphing and interpreting systems of inequalities in this chapter, along with useful examples and thorough explanations.

Two or more disparities taken into consideration collectively constitute a system of inequalities. The set of all points that concurrently meet every inequality is the system's solution. The viable region is a region on the Cartesian plane formed by these points.

Consider the following system of inequalities:

$$y \leq 2x + 1$$
$$y \geq -x + 2$$

To analyze this system, we need to graph each inequality and identify the overlapping region that satisfies both conditions.

Graphing Individual Inequalities

1. Graph $y \leq 2x + 1$:
- Begin by graphing the boundary line $y = 2x + 1$. This line has a slope of 2 and a y-intercept of 1.
- Plot points such as (0, 1) and (1, 3) and draw the line.
- Since the inequality is $\leq$, shade the region below the line.

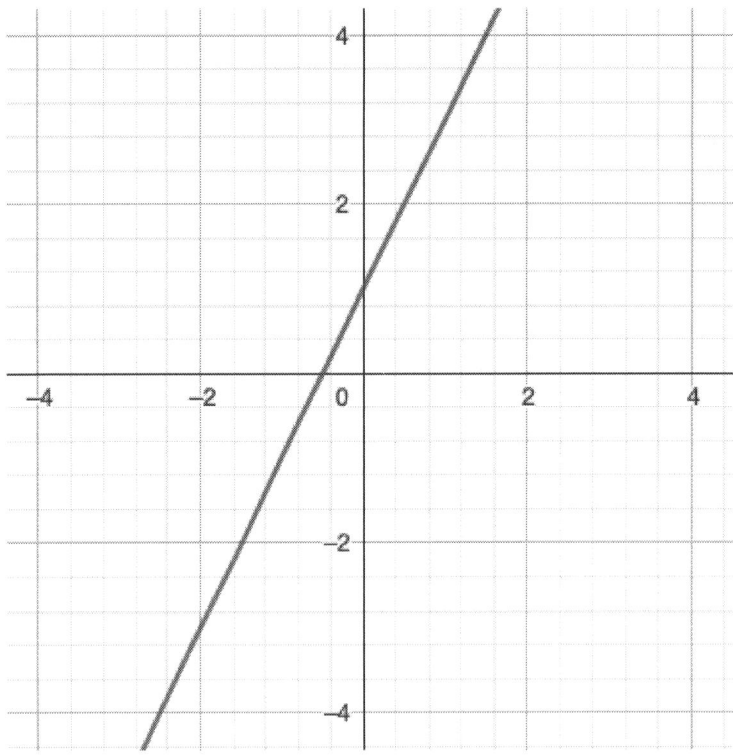

2. Graph $y \geq -x + 2$:
- Begin by graphing the boundary line $y = -x + 2$. This line has a slope of -1 and a y-intercept of 2.
- Plot points such as (0, 2) and (2, 0) and draw the line.
- Since the inequality is $\geq$, shade the region above the line.

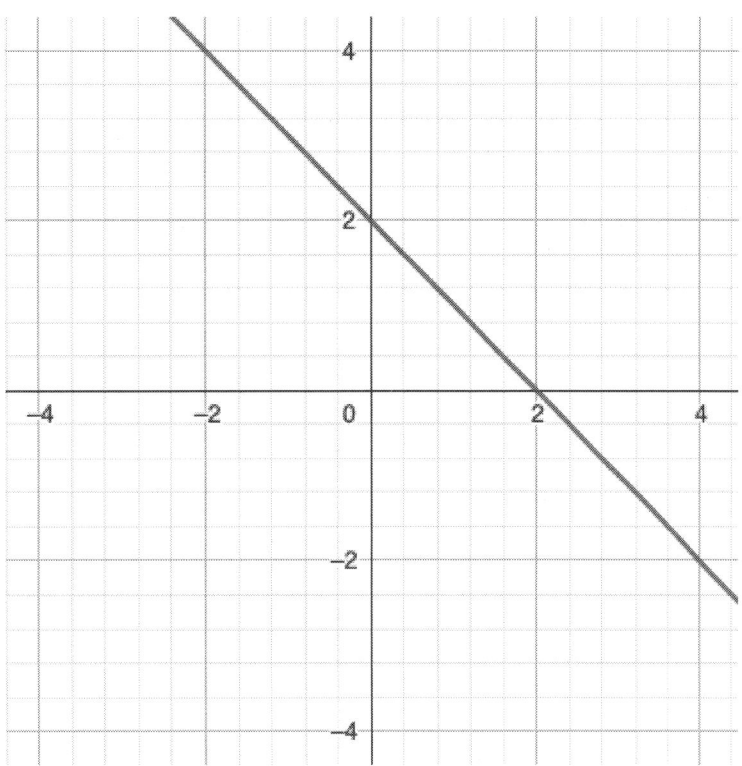

Identifying the Feasible Region

The intersection of the shaded regions representing the individual inequalities is the viable region. All the points that concurrently meet both inequalities are represented by this region. By looking at the spots where the lines connect and the double-shaded areas, one may determine the borders of this region.

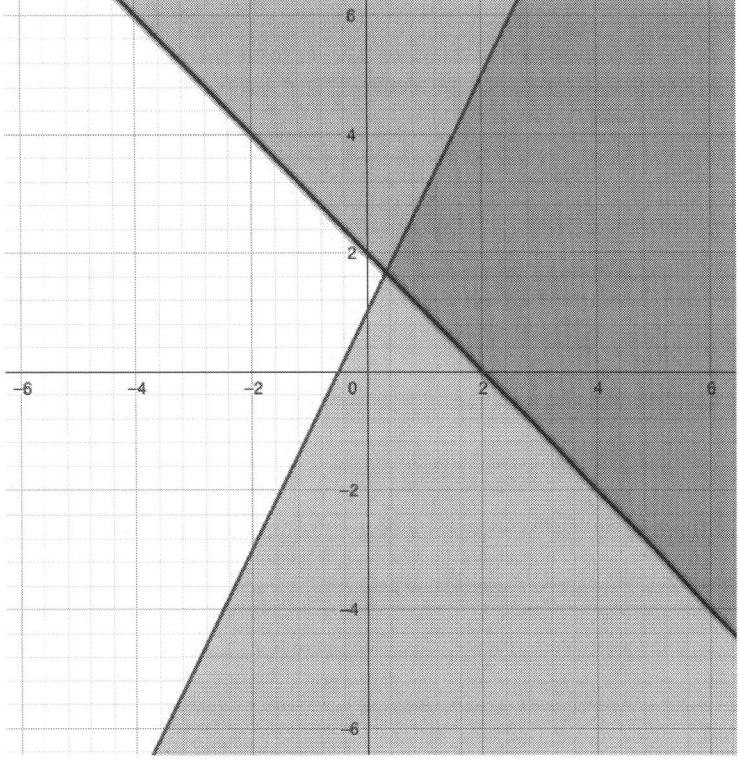

Example: Analyzing a More Complex System

Consider the system:

$$y < 3x - 2$$
$$y \geq -\tfrac{1}{2}x + 1$$
$$x \leq 4$$

To analyze this system, follow these steps:

1. Graph y < 3x - 2:
   - Graph the boundary line y = 3x - 2. This line has a slope of 3 and a y-intercept of -2.
   - Plot points such as (0, -2) and (1, 1) and draw the line.
   - Use a dashed line and shade the area below it because the inequality is <.

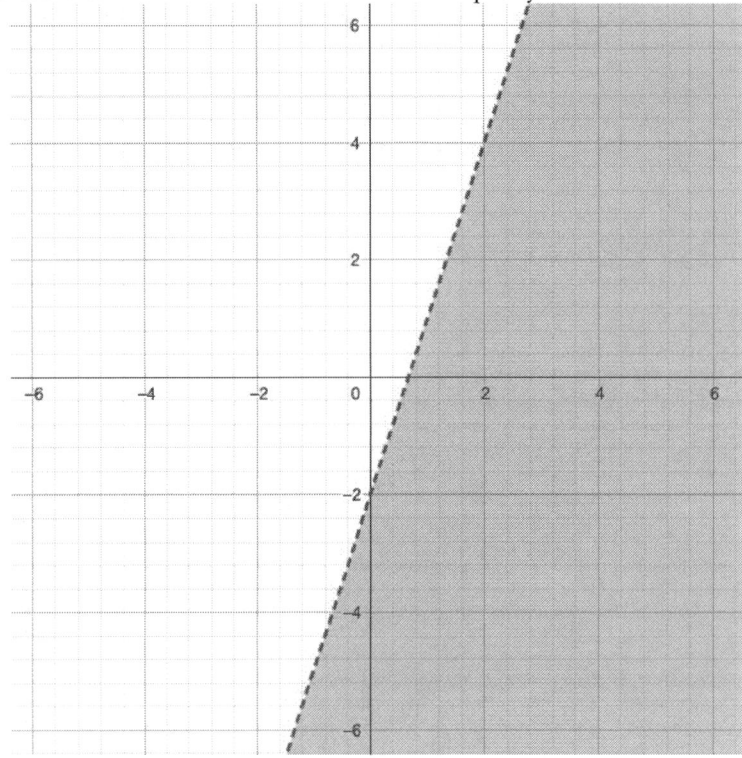

2. Graph $y \geq -\tfrac{1}{2}x + 1$

   - Graph the boundary line $y = -\tfrac{1}{2}x + 1$. This line has a slope of -0.5 and a y-intercept of 1.
   - Plot points such as (0, 1) and (2, 0) and draw the line.
   - As the inequality is ≥, shade the area above the line with a solid line.

3. Graph x ≤ 4:
   - Graph the vertical boundary line x = 4.
   - Given that the inequality is ≤, shade the area to the left of the line with a solid line.

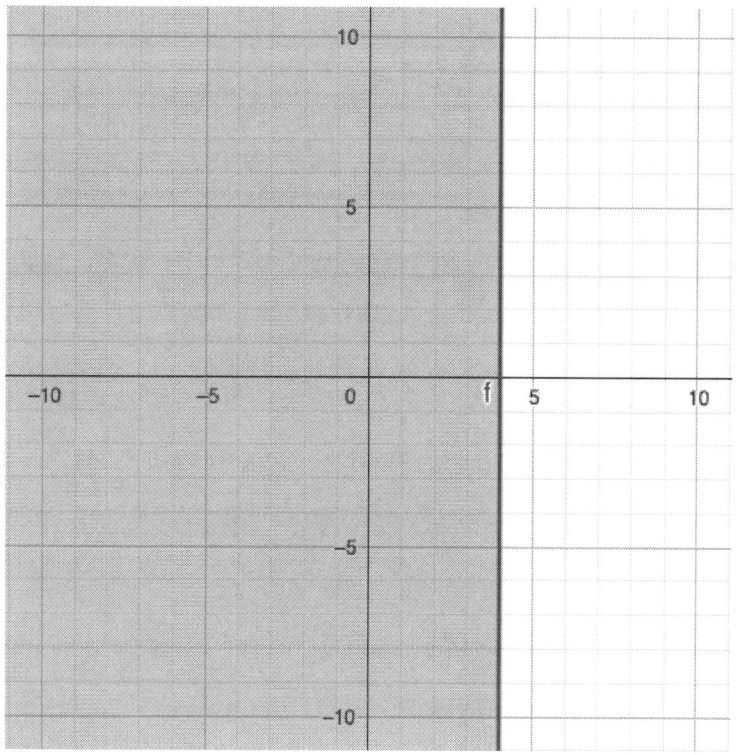

4. Identify the Feasible Region:

- The intersection of all three shaded areas is the feasible region.
- By locating the locations where the boundary lines connect, ascertain the vertices of this area.

Finding Intersection Points

To accurately identify the vertices of the feasible region, solve the equations of the boundary lines where they intersect.

1. Intersection of $y = 3x - 2$ **and** $y = -\frac{1}{2}x + 1$:

- Set the equations equal to each other:

$$3x - 2 = -\frac{1}{2}x + 1$$

- Solve for x:

$$3x + \frac{1}{2}x = 1 + 2$$

$$\frac{7}{2}x = 3$$

$$x = \frac{6}{7}$$

- Substitute \(x \) back into one of the equations to find \(y \):

$$y = 3\left(\frac{6}{7}\right) - 2$$

$$y = \frac{18}{7} - 2$$

$$y = \frac{18}{7} - \frac{14}{7}$$

$$y = \frac{4}{7}$$

Thus, the intersection point is (6/7, 4/7).

35

2. Intersection of y = 3x - 2 and x = 4:
- Substitute x = 4 into y = 3x - 2:

y = 3(4) - 2

y = 12 - 2

y = 10

Thus, the intersection point is (4, 10).

3. Intersection of $y = -\frac{1}{2}x + 1$ and $x = 4$:

- Substitute $x = 4$ into $y = -\frac{1}{2}x + 1$:

$$y = -\frac{1}{2}(4) + 1$$

$$y = -2 + 1$$

$$y = -1$$

Thus, the intersection point is (4, -1).

REAL-WORLD APPLICATIONS OF INEQUALITIES

Knowing inequalities and how to use them outside of the classroom can help with a variety of real-world issues by providing useful tools. We can simulate and solve problems in environmental science, engineering, economics, and everyday decision-making with the aid of inequality. This chapter explores the practical uses of inequality, highlighting its applicability and usefulness in a range of situations.

Inequalities are used to symbolize situations or limitations in actual life. Because these limitations provide a range of workable alternatives rather than a single result, inequalities are especially helpful in feasibility and optimization studies. For example, firms utilize inequalities to optimize revenue while reducing expenses, engineers utilize them to guarantee security and effectiveness in blueprints, and environmental scientists utilize them to handle resources in an environmentally responsible manner.

Economic Applications

When it comes to economic analysis and planning, inequality is vital. They are applied to financial risk assessment, production process optimization, and budget constraint modeling. Consider a company that produces items A and B and has the following restrictions:

- Each unit of product A requires 3 hours of labor, and each unit of product B requires 2 hours of labor. The company has a maximum of 240 labor hours available.
- The cost to produce each unit of product A is $50, and each unit of product B is $30. The company has a budget of $3,000.

These constraints can be modeled using inequalities:

$$3x + 2y \leq 240$$

$$50x + 30y \leq 3000$$

In this case, x stands for the quantity of product A units and y for the quantity of product B units. To find the optimal production levels, we graph these inequalities and determine the feasible region.

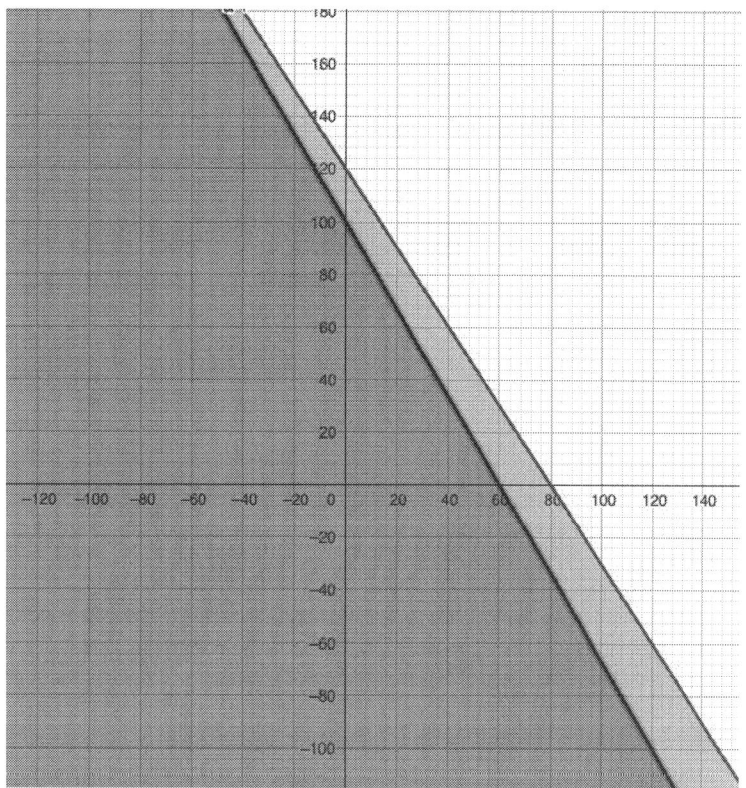

Example: Budget Allocation

Suppose a student has a budget of $200 for textbooks and supplies for the semester. If the price of a textbook is $40 and the price of a supply item is $10, the inequality representing the budget constraint is:

$$40x + 10y \leq 200$$

Where x is the number of textbooks, and y is the number of supply items. By graphing this inequality, the student can determine the possible combinations of textbooks and supplies that fit within the budget.

Engineering Applications

In engineering, inequalities are essential for ensuring that designs meet safety, performance, and cost criteria. Engineers use inequalities to model stress, load, and material constraints in structures and machinery.

Example: Structural Design

Consider a beam that must support a load of up to 5000 pounds without exceeding a stress limit of 1000 pounds per square inch. If the cross-sectional area of the beam is A square inches, the stress inequality is:

$$\frac{Load}{Area} \leq Stress$$
$$\frac{5000}{A} \leq 1000$$

Solving for A, we get:

$$A \geq \frac{5000}{1000}$$
$$A \geq 5$$

Thus, the beam must have a cross-sectional area of at least 5 square inches to safely support the load.

Environmental Science Applications

Environmental scientists use inequalities to model resource constraints and environmental impact. Assessing environmental concerns and developing sustainable management plans for natural resources are made easier by inequality.

Example: Water Resource Management

Assume that a region needs at least 5,000 gallons of water a day for residential, commercial, and agricultural purposes. If a river and a reservoir are the accessible water sources, and the river provides R gallons and the reservoir provides S gallons, then the inequality that represents the water requirement is as follows:

$$R + S \geq 5000$$

Additionally, if the maximum capacity of the reservoir is 3000 gallons, another inequality is:

$$S \leq 3000$$

By solving these inequalities, planners can determine the feasible allocation of water resources to meet daily demands while staying within capacity limits.

Healthcare Applications

Inequalities are employed in the healthcare industry to manage healthcare delivery systems, enhance treatment programs, and allocate resources optimally. Hospitals, for instance, utilize disparities to control staffing levels so they can meet patient needs and labor laws at the same time.

Example: Staff Scheduling

Consider a hospital that needs at least 20 nurses on duty at all times. If the hospital employs full-time nurses F who work 8-hour shifts and part-time nurses P who work 4-hour shifts, the inequality representing the staffing requirement is:

$$8F + 4P \geq 160$$

Where 160 is the total number of nursing hours needed per day (20 nurses x 8 hours). This inequality helps the hospital ensure adequate staffing levels while optimizing nurse schedules.

Formulating and Solving Inequality Problems

Formulating inequality problems requires translating real-world conditions into mathematical expressions. Graphing the inequalities, locating the feasible region, and selecting the best solution are frequently required steps in solving these problems.

Example: Profit Maximization

A small business produces two types of handmade crafts, A and B. The profit from each craft A is $15, and from each craft B is $20. The production constraints are as follows:

- Each craft A requires 2 hours of labor, and each craft B requires 3 hours of labor. The total labor available is 120 hours.
- The materials for each craft A cost $5, and for each craft B cost $7. The total budget for materials is $140.

The inequalities representing these constraints are:

$$2x + 3y \leq 120$$

$$5x + 7y \leq 140$$

Where x represents the number of crafts A, and y represents the number of crafts B. The profit function to be maximized is:

P = 15x + 20y

1. Graph the Inequalities:

$$2x + 3y \leq 120$$

$$5x + 7y \leq 140$$

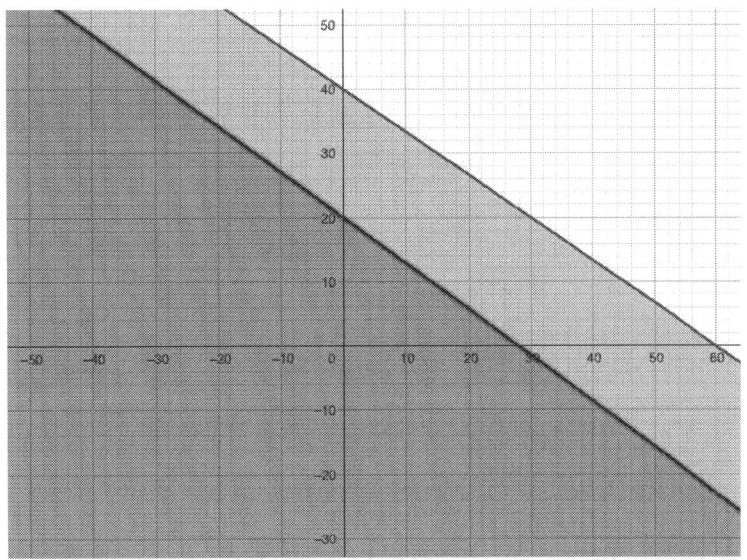

2. Identify the Feasible Region:
   - Locate the spots where the boundary lines connect to find the vertices of the viable region.

3. Calculate Profit at Each Vertex:
   - To determine the highest profit, analyze the profit function P = 15x + 20y at each vertex of the viable zone.

By analyzing the system of inequalities and calculating the profit at each feasible point, the business can determine the optimal production levels of crafts A and B to maximize profit.

CHAPTER 6: LINEAR FUNCTIONS

UNDERSTANDING FUNCTION NOTATION

Functions are essential for characterizing the connections between variables in the field of algebra. For students getting ready for the Digital SAT®, function notation—a succinct approach to depict these relationships—is a vital concept. Accurate and timely issue solving requires an understanding of function notation interpretation and manipulation. With thorough explanations and useful examples, this chapter offers a thorough overview of function notation.

Every input has exactly one output when it comes to a function. It can be shown in a number of methods, such as verbal explanations, tables, diagrams, and equations. Function notation provides a standardized way to denote functions, making it easier to communicate and work with them.

The most widely used notation for functions is $f(x)$, where x is the input variable and f is the function's name. When x is the input, the function's output is represented by the expression $f(x)$.

Think about the function:

$f(x) = 2x + 3$

In this instance, $f(x)$ is a function whose output is produced by multiplying the input value by two and then adding three.

Interpreting Function Notation

It is essential to comprehend the functions of the input and output variables in order to interpret function notation. The input variable, sometimes referred to as the independent variable, is the value that you enter into the function. The output variable, sometimes referred to as the dependent variable, is what results from applying the function rule to the input.

For example, given $f(x) = 2x + 3$:

- If $x = 1$, then $f(1) = 2(1) + 3 = 5$.

- If $x = -2$, then $f(-2) = 2(-2) + 3 = -1$.

These calculations show how the function produces different outputs based on the inputs.

Evaluating Functions

A function's evaluation entails changing the input variable to a specified value and figuring out the matching output. Though simple in nature, this technique demands close attention to detail.

Consider the function:

$g(x) = x^2 - 4x + 7$

To evaluate g(x) at different values of x:

- For $x = 0, g(0) = (0)^2 - 4(0) + 7 = 7$.

- For $x = 2, g(2) = (2)^2 - 4(2) + 7 = 4 - 8 + 7 = 3$.

- For $x = -3, g(-3) = (-3)^2 - 4(-3) + 7 = 9 + 12 + 7 = 28$.

These examples illustrate the process of function evaluation, which is essential for solving problems involving functions on the Digital SAT®.

Domain and Range

The set of all potential input values is known as a function's domain, while the set of all possible output values is known as its range. It is essential to comprehend a function's domain and range in order to properly interpret and graph it.

Consider the function:

$$h(x) = \frac{1}{x-2}$$

Find the values of x that cause the function to become undefined in order to ascertain the domain. In this case, h(x) is undefined when x = 2, as division by zero is not possible. So, with the exception of x = 2, the domain is all real numbers:

Domain: $x \neq 2$

To find the range, analyze the possible outputs. For h(x), the output can take any real value except 0, as there is no x that makes the numerator 0. Thus, the range is all real numbers except 0:

Range: $y \neq 0$

Graphing Functions

Graphing a function involves plotting points that represent input-output pairs and connecting them to visualize the relationship. This graphical depiction aids in comprehending how the function behaves.

Consider the function:

$$f(x) = -x^2 + 4x - 3$$

To graph f(x), follow these steps:

1. Identify key points by evaluating the function at specific values of x:

- For $x = 0$, $f(0) = -(0)^2 + 4(0) - 3 = -3$.

- For $x = 1$, $f(1) = -(1)^2 + 4(1) - 3 = -1 + 4 - 3 = 0$.

- For $x = 2$, $f(2) = -(2)^2 + 4(2) - 3 = -4 + 8 - 3 = 1$.

2. Plot these points on the Cartesian plane:
(0, -3)
(1, 0)
(2, 1)

3. To finish the graph, join the points with a gentle curve.

Operations with Functions

Functions can be combined and manipulated through various operations, including addition, subtraction, multiplication, and division. These operations create new functions from existing ones.

Consider two functions:

$$f(x) = x + 2$$
$$g(x) = 3x - 1$$

1. Addition:

$$(f + g)(x) = f(x) + g(x) = (x + 2) + (3x - 1) = 4x + 1$$

2. Subtraction:

$$(f - g)(x) = f(x) - g(x) = (x + 2) - (3x - 1) = x + 2 - 3x + 1 = -2x + 3$$

3. Multiplication:

$$(f \cdot g)(x) = f(x) \cdot g(x) = (x + 2)(3x - 1) = 3x^2 - x + 6x - 2 = 3x^2 + 5x - 2$$

4. Division:

$$\left(\frac{f}{g}\right)(x) = \frac{f(x)}{g(x)} = \frac{x+2}{3x-1}$$

These operations demonstrate how new functions can be derived from existing ones, expanding the range of problems that can be solved.

Composite Functions

Applying one function to a function's result is known as composite functions. The notation for a composite function is $(f \circ g)(x)$, which means f(g(x)).

Consider two functions:

$$f(x) = 2x + 3$$
$$g(x) = x^2 - 1$$

To find the composite function $(f \circ g)(x)$
1. Substitute g(x) into f(x):

$$(f \circ g)(x) = f(g(x)) = f(x^2 - 1)$$

2. Apply the function f:

$$f(x^2 - 1) = 2(x^2 - 1) + 3 = 2x^2 - 2 + 3 = 2x^2 + 1$$

Thus, $(f \circ g)(x) = 2x^2 + 1$.

Inverse Functions

An inverse function maps the output back to the input in order to undo the effects of the original function. If $f(x)$ is a function, its inverse is denoted by $f^{-1}(x)$.

The procedures below can be used to determine a function's inverse:
1. Replace $f(x)$ with y:
   $y = f(x)$
2. Swap x and y:
   $x = f(y)$
3. Solve for y to express it in terms of x:
   $y = f^{-1}(x)$

Consider the function:

$$f(x) = \frac{x-3}{2}$$

To find its inverse:
1. Replace $f(x)$ with y:

$$y = \frac{x-3}{2}$$

2. Swap x and y:

$$x = \frac{y-3}{2}$$

3. Solve for y:
   2x = y - 3
   y = 2x + 3

Thus, the inverse function is $f^{-1}(x) = 2x + 3$.

PLOTTING LINEAR FUNCTIONS

An essential part of algebra are linear functions, which depict connections with constant rates of change. Comprehending the plotting of these functions is essential for illustrating their behavior and resolving related issues. We will examine graphing methods for linear functions in this chapter, along with thorough explanations and useful examples. A linear function can be expressed using the formula y = mx + b, where m is the slope and b is the y-intercept. The y-intercept (b) is a representation of the point on the y-axis where the line crosses it, and the slope (m) shows how quickly the function changes.

Understanding the Slope-Intercept Form
The most widely used form for representing a linear function is the slope-intercept form, which is y = mx + b. It provides an immediate understanding of the function's characteristics:
- The slope m indicates the steepness and direction of the line.
- The line's beginning on the y-axis is indicated by the y-intercept b.

Example: Interpreting a Linear Function
Consider the function:
y = 2x + 3

In this equation:
- The slope m = 2 indicates that for every unit increase in x, y increases by 2 units.
- When the line intersects the y-axis at (0, 3), it is said to have a y-intercept of 3.

Plotting the Function
To plot the linear function y = 2x + 3, follow these steps:
1. **Identify the y-Intercept**: Start by plotting the y-intercept (0, 3) on the graph.
2. **Use the Slope**: Utilize the slope to determine another point from the y-intercept. Given that the slope is 2, shift the x- and y-axes in positive directions by one and two units, respectively. The point is therefore given (1, 5).
3. **Draw the Line**: Draw a straight line connecting the two spots that extends in both directions.

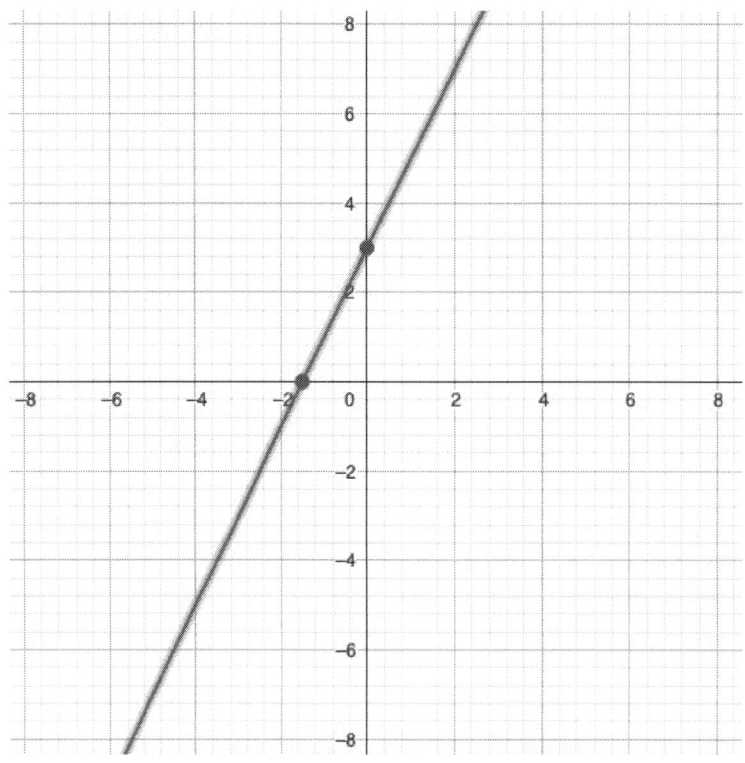

Different Forms of Linear Equations

Although the slope-intercept form is often utilized, there are alternative ways to write linear equations, including the point-slope form and the standard form.

Point-Slope Form

When you are aware of both the slope of the line and a particular point along it, the point-slope form comes in handy. The formula is as follows: $y - y1 = m(x - x1)$, where m is the slope and $(x1, y1)$ is a point on the line.

Example: Using the Point-Slope Form

Given a point (3, 4) and a slope of 2, the equation of the line is:
$y - 4 = 2(x - 3)$

To convert this to slope-intercept form:
$y - 4 = 2x - 6$
$y = 2x - 6 + 4$
$y = 2x - 2$

This confirms that the line has a slope of 2 and passes through the point (3, 4).

Standard Form

A linear equation has the conventional form $Ax + By = C$, where A, B, and C are constants.

Example: Converting to Standard Form

Convert the slope-intercept form $y = 2x + 3$ to standard form:
$y = 2x + 3$
$-2x + y = 3$
$2x - y = -3$

This is the standard form of the equation, where $A = 2$, $B = -1$, and $C = -3$.

Graphing Linear Equations in Standard Form

Determine the x- and y-intercepts of a linear equation in standard form to graph it:
- Where the line crosses the x-axis (y = 0) is known as the x-intercept.
- Where the line crosses the y-axis (x = 0) is known as the y-intercept.

Example: Graphing from Standard Form

Consider the equation:

$3x + 4y = 12$

1.*Find the y-Intercept: Set x = 0 :

$3(0) + 4y = 12$

$4y = 12$

$y = 3$

The y-intercept is (0, 3).

2. Find the x-Intercept: Set y = 0):

$3x + 4(0) = 12$

$3x = 12$

$x = 4$

The x-intercept is (4, 0).

3. Plot the Points: Plot the intercepts (0, 3) and (4, 0) on the graph.

4. Draw the Line: Connect the points with a straight line.

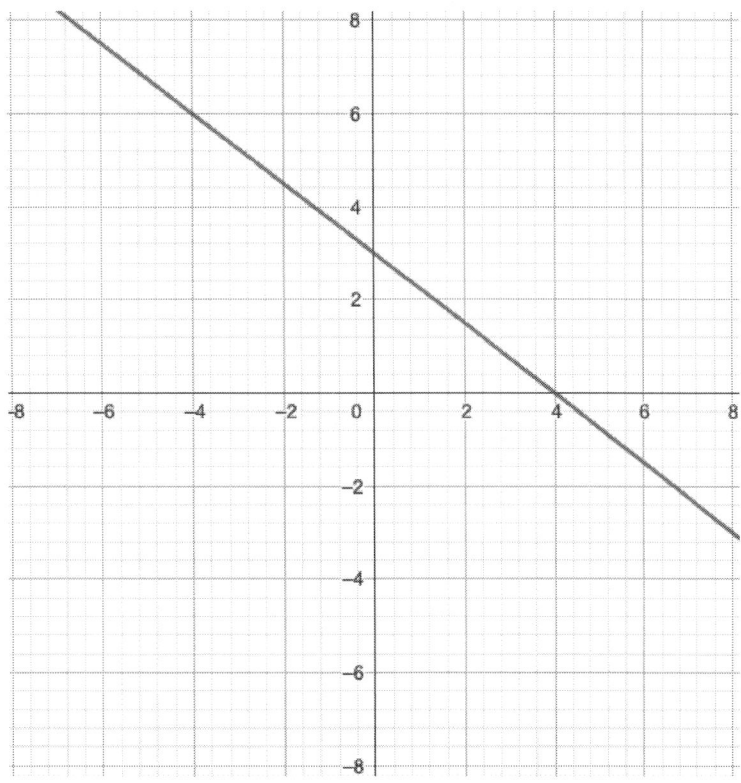

Slope of a Line

A line's steepness and direction can be determined by looking at its slope. The ratio of the vertical change to the horizontal change between two points on the line is used to calculate it.

$$\text{Slope} = \frac{\Delta y}{\Delta x} = \frac{y_2 - y_1}{x_2 - x_1}$$

Example: Calculating Slope

Given two points (2, 3) and (5, 7), calculate the slope of the line:

$$m = \frac{7-3}{5-2} = \frac{4}{3}$$

The slope m = 4/3 indicates that for every 3 units the line moves horizontally, it moves 4 units vertically.

Horizontal, Vertical, Parallel and Perpendicular Lines

Horizontal and vertical lines have unique characteristics:

- A horizontal line has a slope of 0 and is represented by y = b.
- A vertical line, denoted by x = a, has an unknown slope.
- The slopes of parallel and perpendicular lines are the negative reciprocals of one another, although the y-intercepts of parallel and perpendicular lines differ.

CHAPTER 7: RATE, RATIO, PERCENTAGE, PROPORTION, AND UNITS

UNDERSTADING RATES

Rates are an essential concept in mathematics because they quantify the relationship between one quantity and another. They are widely employed in many disciplines, such as economics, science, and daily life. Comprehending rates is essential for students getting ready for the Digital SAT® because it enables them to work through challenges pertaining to density, speed, cost per unit, and other rate-related ideas. This chapter explores the idea of rates, including definitions, uses, and approaches to associated problems.

A ratio that contrasts two distinct quantities expressed in several units is called a rate. The amount of interest is represented by the numerator, which is stated as a fraction, while the unit of comparison is represented by the denominator. The general form of a rate is:

Rate = Quantity/Unit

For example, the speed of a car can be expressed as a rate:

Speed = Distance/Time

If a car travels 60 miles in 2 hours, its speed is:

Speed} = 60 miles/2 hours = 30 miles per hour (mph)

Types of Rates

There are various types of rates used in different contexts. Some common types include:

1. Speed: Measures how fast an object moves over a certain distance in a specific amount of time.
   Speed = Distance/Time
2. Density: Measures mass per unit volume.
   Density = Mass/Volume
3. Flow Rate: Determines how much fluid flows through a spot in a given amount of time.
   Flow Rate = Volume/Time
4. Cost per Unit: Calculates the price for a product's single unit.
   Cost per Unit = Total Cost/Number of Units

Example: Calculating Speed

Consider a runner who completes a 10-kilometer race in 40 minutes. To calculate the runner's speed in kilometers per minute (km/min), use the formula for speed:

Speed = Distance/Time

Speed = 10 km/40 min = 0.25 km/min

To convert this speed to kilometers per hour (km/h):

Speed = 0.25 km/min x 60 min/hour = 15 km/h

Example: Calculating Density

Suppose a block of metal has a mass of 200 grams and a volume of 50 cubic centimeters. To calculate the density, use the formula:

Density = Mass/Volume

Density = $200g/50cm^3$ = 4 g/cm^3

Example: Calculating Flow Rate

A water tank dispenses 500 liters of water in 5 minutes. To calculate the flow rate in liters per minute (L/min), use the formula:

Flow Rate = Volume/Time

Flow Rate = 500 L/5 min = 100 L/min

Solving Problems Involving Rates

When solving problems involving rates, it is essential to carefully analyze the given information and use the appropriate formulas. Some steps to take are as follows:

1. **Identify the Quantities**: Determine the quantities involved and their units.
2. **Write the Rate**: Express the rate as a fraction.
3. **Convert Units**: If necessary, convert the units to make calculations easier.
4. **Solve for the Unknown**: Use algebraic techniques to solve for the unknown quantity.

Example: Calculating Cost per Unit

A company purchases 1,200 widgets for $3,600. To calculate the cost per widget, use the formula:

Cost per Unit = Total Cost/Number of Units

Cost per Unit = 3600 dollars/1200 widgets = 3 dollars/widget

Example: Rate of Change

Rates can also be used to describe how a quantity changes over time, known as the rate of change. Consider a population of bacteria that grows from 1,000 to 2,500 in 5 hours. To calculate the rate of change:

Rate of Change = Change in Quantity/Time

Rate of Change = (2500 − 1000)/5 hours = 1500/5 hours = 300 bacteria/hour

Advanced Applications of Rates

Rates are not only useful for simple calculations but also for more complex applications in various fields. Here are some advanced examples:

Physics

In physics, rates are used to describe motion, energy transfer, and other phenomena. For example, acceleration is the rate of change of velocity over time:

Acceleration = Change in Velocity/Time

Example: Calculating Acceleration

A car accelerates from 0 to 60 miles per hour in 8 seconds. To calculate the acceleration:

Acceleration = (60 mph - 0 mph)/8 seconds = 60 mph/8 seconds

To convert to meters per second squared (m/s^2), use the conversion factor 1 mph -> approx 0.44704 m/s:

Acceleration = (60 x 0.44704 m/s)/8 seconds -> approx 3.35 m/s^2

Economics

In economics, rates are used to analyze growth, inflation, and interest. An important idea is the interest rate, which indicates the return on investment or the cost of borrowing money.

Example: Calculating Interest

To calculate simple interest:

Interest = Principal x Rate x Time

If $1,000 is invested at an annual interest rate of 5% for 3 years:

Interest = 1000 x 0.05 x 3 = 150 dollars

Medicine

In medicine, rates are used to describe dosages, metabolic rates, and other biological processes. The metabolic rate measures the amount of energy expended per unit time.

Example: Calculating Metabolic Rate

If a person burns 2,000 calories in a day, their metabolic rate can be expressed as:

Metabolic Rate = 2000 calories/24 hours -> approx 83.33 calories/hour

Students can tackle a variety of difficulties in a variety of academic subjects by grasping the idea of rates and their applications. Comprehending rates is crucial not only for achieving success on the Digital SAT® but also for real-world applications in numerous professional domains and daily life.

WORKING WITH RATIOS AND PROPORTIONS

The mathematical ideas of ratios and proportions are foundational and have numerous applications in science, engineering, finance, and daily life. Since ratios and proportions are commonly used in the math section of the exam, it is imperative that students prepare for the Digital SAT® by having a solid understanding of these concepts. This chapter offers a thorough examination of ratios and proportions, covering their definitions, characteristics, and real-world uses. The division of two quantities for comparison is called a ratio. It conveys the relative amount of one quantity to another. Three formats can be used to write ratios:

1. **As a fraction**: a/b
2. **With a colon**: a:b
3. **In words**: "a to b"

For example, if there are 4 apples and 3 oranges in a basket, the ratio of apples to oranges can be expressed as: 4/3, 4:3, or 4 to 3

Properties of Ratios

Ratios have several important properties that make them useful for solving problems:

1. **Equivalent Ratios**: If the value of two ratios is the same when they are simplified, they are equivalent. For instance, since both ratios reduce to the same value, 4/6 and 2/3 are equivalent.
2. **Scaling Ratios**: It's possible to multiply or divide each terms by the same number to scale a ratio up or down. For instance, by multiplying both terms by 2, one can increase the ratio 2/3 to 4/6.

Example: Simplifying Ratios

Consider the ratio 8/12. To simplify this ratio, divide both terms by their greatest common divisor (GCD), which is 4:

$$\frac{8 \div 4}{12 \div 4} = \frac{2}{3}$$

Introduction to Proportions

A proportion is an equation that states that two ratios are equal. It can be written in the form: a/b = c/d

Proportions are used to solve problems involving equivalent ratios. The key property of proportions is that the cross-products are equal:

$$a \cdot d = b \cdot c$$

Example: Solving a Proportion

Consider the proportion:
¾ = x/8

To solve for x, use the cross-multiplication property:

$$3 \cdot 8 = 4 \cdot x$$

$$24 = 4x$$

$$x = \frac{24}{4}$$

$$x = 6$$

Practical Applications of Ratios and Proportions

Ratios and proportions are widely used in various real-life scenarios, including recipe adjustments, map reading, and financial analysis.

Example: Adjusting a Recipe

Suppose a recipe calls for 2 cups of flour and 3 cups of sugar to make 12 cookies. To make 18 cookies, determine the amount of flour needed using a proportion:

2 cups of flour/12 cookies = x cups of flour/18 cookies

Cross-multiply to solve for x:

$$2 \cdot 18 = 12 \cdot x$$

$$36 = 12x$$

$$x = \frac{36}{12}$$

$$x = 3 \text{ cups of flour}$$

Example: Map Reading

Maps often use a scale to represent real-world distances. If a map scale indicates that 1 inch represents 5 miles, find the actual distance between two points that are 3 inches apart on the map:

1 inch/5 miles = 3 inches/x miles

Cross-multiply to solve for x:

$$1 \cdot x = 5 \cdot 3$$

$$x = 15 \text{ miles}$$

Example: Financial Analysis

In finance, ratios are used to analyze the performance and stability of companies. For example, the debt-to-equity ratio compares a company's total debt to its shareholder equity:

Debt-to-Equity Ratio = Total Debt / Shareholder Equity

If a company has $750,000 in total debt and $2,500,000 in shareholder equity, its debt-to-equity ratio is:

Debt-to-Equity Ratio = 750,000 / 2,500,000 = 0.3

Working with Complex Ratios

Complex ratios involve more than two terms or nested ratios. They require careful simplification and manipulation to solve.

Example: Nested Ratios

Consider the ratio:

(3/4)/(5/6)

To simplify, multiply by the reciprocal of the denominator:

$$\frac{3}{4} \div \frac{5}{6} = \frac{3}{4} \times \frac{6}{5} = \frac{3 \cdot 6}{4 \cdot 5} = \frac{18}{20} = \frac{9}{10}$$

Example: Ratios with Multiple Terms

Consider the ratio of three quantities a, b, and c. If the ratio a:b = 2:3 and b:c = 4:5, find the ratio a:b:c.

First, express the ratios with a common term:

$$a : b = 2 : 3 \implies a = 2k \text{ and } b = 3k$$

$$b : c = 4 : 5 \implies b = 4m \text{ and } c = 5m$$

Since both expressions for b must be equal:

3k = 4m

k = 4m/3

Substitute k into the expressions for a and b:

$$a = 2k = 2\left(\frac{4m}{3}\right) = \frac{8m}{3}$$
$$b = 3k = 3\left(\frac{4m}{3}\right) = 4m$$
$$c = 5m$$

Thus, the ratio a:b:c is:

$$a : b : c = \frac{8m}{3} : 4m : 5m$$

Simplify by multiplying each term by 3:
a:b:c = 8:12:15

Ratios in Geometry
Ratios are often used in geometry to compare lengths, areas, and volumes.

Example: Similar Triangles
The ratios of the matching side lengths of identical triangles are equal. Two comparable triangles with side lengths of 3, 4, 5, and 6, 8, 10 should be examined. The ratio of the side lengths is:
3/6 = 1/2
4/8 = 1/2
5/10 = 1/2

Example: Areas and Volumes
The ratio of the areas of two similar figures is the square of the ratio of their corresponding side lengths. The cube of the ratio of two identical solids' respective side lengths equals the ratio of their volumes.

CONVERTING UNITS

A key ability in science and mathematics is unit conversion, which enables us to compare and comprehend quantities measured in various units. To solve issues and comprehend the world around us, precisely converting units is crucial, whether working with weights, volumes, distances, or other quantities. We will examine the fundamentals and strategies of unit conversion in this chapter, using real-world examples and thorough explanations to guarantee a thorough understanding of the subject.

Converting a measurement between different units is known as unit conversion. Numerous disciplines, including science, engineering, medicine, and daily living, depend on this process. Understanding the relationships between various units and being able to use conversion factors effectively are prerequisites for unit conversion.

Basic Principles of Unit Conversion
1. **Identify the Units**: Determine the units you are converting from and to.
2. **Conversion Factors**: Use known conversion factors that relate the units.
3. **Multiply or Divide**: Apply the conversion factor by multiplying or dividing as appropriate.
4. **Dimensional Analysis**: Ensure that units cancel appropriately, leaving the desired unit.

Example: Converting Length
Consider converting 5 kilometers to meters. The conversion factor between kilometers and meters is:
1 kilometer = 1000 meters
To convert 5 kilometers to meters:
5 km x (1000 m/1 km) = 5000 m

Example: Converting Time

Convert 3 hours to seconds. The relationship between hours, minutes, and seconds is:

1 hour = 60 minutes

1 minute = 60 seconds

To convert 3 hours to seconds:

$$3 \text{ hours} \times \frac{60 \text{ minutes}}{1 \text{ hour}} \times \frac{60 \text{ seconds}}{1 \text{ minute}} = 3 \times 60 \times 60 = 10,800 \text{ seconds}$$

Example: Converting Weight

Convert 250 grams to kilograms. The formula to convert grams to kilograms is as follows:

1 kilogram = 1000 grams

To convert 250 grams to kilograms:

250 g x (1 kg/1000 g) = 0.25 kg

Complex Unit Conversions

Complex unit conversions involve multiple steps or converting between units that are not directly related. These require careful application of conversion factors and dimensional analysis.

Example: Converting Speed

90 km/h can be converted to meters per second. The relationships are:

1 kilometer = 1000 meters

1 hour = 3600 seconds

To convert 90 kilometers per hour to meters per second:

$$90 \text{ km/h} \times \frac{1000 \text{ m}}{1 \text{ km}} \times \frac{1 \text{ hour}}{3600 \text{ seconds}} = \frac{90 \times 1000}{3600} \text{ m/s}$$
$$= \frac{90,000}{3600} \text{ m/s}$$
$$= 25 \text{ m/s}$$

Example: Converting Volume

Convert 2 liters to cubic centimeters. The conversion factor between liters and cubic centimeters is:

1 liter = 1000 cubic centimeters (cm^3)

To convert 2 liters to cubic centimeters:

2 L x (1000 cm^3/1 L) = 2000 cm^3

Example: Converting Area

Convert 5 square meters to square centimeters. The relationship between meters and centimeters is:

1 meter = 100 centimeters

Since area is a two-dimensional measure:

1 m^2 = (100 cm)^2 = 10,000 cm^2

To convert 5 square meters to square centimeters:

5 m^2 x (10,000 cm^2/1 m^2 = 50,000 cm^2

Advanced Unit Conversions

Advanced unit conversions may involve converting between compound units or using scientific notation.

Example: Converting Pressure

Convert 2 atmospheres to pascals. The conversion factor is:

1 atmosphere = 101,325 pascals (Pa)

To convert 2 atmospheres to pascals:

2 atm x (101,325 Pa/1 atm) = 202,650 Pa

Example: Scientific Notation

Convert 0.00056 kilograms to grams using scientific notation. The conversion factor is:

1 kilogram = 1000 grams

$0.00056 \text{ kg} = 0.00056 \times 10^3 \text{ g} = 5.6 \times 10^{-1} \text{ g}$

MASTERING PERCENTAGES

The concept of percentages is essential to mathematics and has many applications, ranging from daily life to higher education. Students preparing for the Digital SAT® need to understand percentages and how they are used because they are often used in a variety of problem-solving scenarios. This chapter explores percentages in depth, going into their definitions, computations, and real-world uses.

Using a percentage, one can express a number as a fraction of 100. The Latin "per centum," which meaning "by the hundred," is where the English term "percent" first appeared. To compare amounts, explain changes, and convey information in a consistent manner, percentages are utilized. The basic formula for calculating a percentage is:

Percentage = (Part/Whole) x 100

For example, if 20 out of 50 students in a class are female, the percentage of female students is:

Percentage = (20/50) x 100 = 40%

Calculating Percentages

To calculate percentages, it is essential to understand three key components: the part, the whole, and the percentage. Depending on the given information, different formulas can be applied:

1. **Finding the Percentage**: Use the following formula, given the part and the whole:
   Percentage = (Part/Whole) x 100
2. **Finding the Part**: Apply the following formula, given the whole and the percentage:
   Part = (Percentage/100) x Whole
3. **Finding the Whole**: Given the part and the percentage, use the formula:
   Whole = (Part/Percentage) x 100

Example: Finding the Percentage

If a student scores 85 out of 100 on a test, the percentage score is calculated as follows:

Percentage = (85/100) x 100 = 85%

Example: Finding the Part

If 60% of a 200-page book has been read, the number of pages read is calculated as follows:

Part = (60/100) x 200 = 120 pages

Example: Finding the Whole

If 25% of a quantity is 50, the total quantity is calculated as follows:

Whole = (50/25) x 100 = 200

Converting Between Decimals, Fractions, and Percentages

Understanding the relationship between decimals, fractions, and percentages is crucial for solving problems efficiently. Converting between these forms allows for easier calculations and comparisons.

1. **Fraction to Percentage**: Multiply the fraction by 100.
   Percentage = (a/b) x 100
2. **Decimal to Percentage**: Multiply the decimal by 100.
   Percentage = Decimal x 100
3. **Percentage to Fraction**: Divide the percentage by 100 and simplify if necessary.
   Fraction = Percentage/100
4. **Percentage to Decimal**: Divide the percentage by 100.
   Decimal = Percentage/100

Example: Converting a Fraction to a Percentage
Convert 3/4 to a percentage:
(3/4) x 100 = 75%

Example: Converting a Decimal to a Percentage
Convert 0.85 to a percentage:
0.85 x 100 = 85%

Example: Converting a Percentage to a Fraction
Convert 40% to a fraction:
40/100 = 2/5

Example: Converting a Percentage to a Decimal
Convert 25% to a decimal:
25/100 = 0.25

Applications of Percentages
Percentages are used in a variety of real-world applications, including finance, statistics, and everyday calculations.

Calculating Interest
To calculate simple interest, use the formula:
Interest = Principal x Rate x Time
If $1,000 is invested at an annual interest rate of 5% for 3 years, the interest earned is:
Interest = 1000 x 0.05 x 3 = 150 dollars

Calculating Discounts
Simply deduct the discount percentage from the original price to find the discounted price of an item.
If a $200 item is on sale for 20% off, the discount amount is:
Discount Amount = 200 x 0.20 = 40 dollars
Discounted Price} = 200 - 40 = 160 dollars

Calculating Proportions
If 250 out of 1,000 survey respondents prefer a particular product, the percentage of respondents who prefer the product is:
(250/1000) x 100 = 25%

Calculating Tips
To calculate a tip at a restaurant, multiply the bill amount by the tip percentage.
If the bill is $50 and you want to leave a 15% tip:
Tip Amount = 50 x 0.15 = 7.50 dollars

Calculating Sales Tax
Add the sales tax percentage to the initial price of an item to determine its total cost with sales tax applied.
If an item costs $100 and the sales tax rate is 8%:
Tax Amount = 100 x 0.08 = 8 dollars
Total Cos} = 100 + 8 = 108 dollars

Calculating Compound Interest
Interest accrued over prior periods is computed in addition to the original principal when compound interest is applied. The following is the compound interest formula:

$$A = P\left(1 + \frac{r}{n}\right)^{nt}$$

where:

- A is the entire sum of money, interest comprised, that has accumulated after n years.
- P stands for principal, or the starting sum of money.
- r is the yearly interest rate, expressed in decimal.
- n is the annual compounding frequency of interest.
- t is the period of the money invested, stated in years.

Example: Calculating Compound Interest*

If $1,000 is invested at an annual interest rate of 5%, compounded quarterly for 3 years:

$$A = 1000 \left(1 + \frac{0.05}{4}\right)^{4 \times 3}$$
$$= 1000 \left(1 + 0.0125\right)^{12}$$
$$= 1000 \left(1.0125\right)^{12}$$
$$= 1000 \times 1.1616$$
$$= 1161.60 \text{ dollars}$$

Calculating Percentage Change

Percentage change measures the degree of change over time. The formula for percentage change is:

$$\text{Percentage Change} = \left(\frac{\text{New Value} - \text{Old Value}}{\text{Old Value}}\right) \times 100$$

Example: Calculating Percentage Change

If a stock price increases from $50 to $65:

$$\text{Percentage Change} = \left(\frac{65 - 50}{50}\right) \times 100 = 30\%$$

Calculating Weighted Averages

A weighted average takes into account the relative importance of each value. The formula for a weighted average is:

$$\text{Weighted Average} = \frac{\sum(w_i \times x_i)}{\sum w_i}$$

where:

- w_i are the weights.
- x_i are the values.

Example: Calculating Weighted Averages

If a student's grades are weighted as follows: Homework (20%), Quizzes (30%), Exams (50%), with scores of 85, 90, and 80 respectively:

$$\text{Weighted Average} = \frac{(0.20 \times 85) + (0.30 \times 90) + (0.50 \times 80)}{0.20 + 0.30 + 0.50}$$
$$= \frac{17 + 27 + 40}{1}$$
$$= 84$$

CHAPTER 8: DATA INTERPRETATION AND STATISTICS

ANALYZING TABLES AND GRAPHS

Analyzing tables and graphs is a basic skill that students studying for the Digital SAT® need to have. We are able to rapidly comprehend complex information and recognize trends, patterns, and relationships because to these visual representations of data. In order to guarantee that students gain a solid understanding of how to interpret tables and graphs, this chapter covers the fundamentals of this subject and offers helpful examples and thorough explanations.

It is easier to comprehend and analyze data when it is represented using tables and graphs. While graphs offer a visual interpretation that can reveal insights not immediately evident in numerical form, tables deliver facts in a methodical manner. Success in a variety of disciplines, such as the social sciences, sciences, and economics, depends on having mastered these instruments.

Data is shown in rows and columns in tables, which facilitates the comparison of various data sets. Recognizing the labels, units of measurement, and connections between data items are essential to reading and interpreting tables.

Example: Reading a Simple Table
Consider a table showing the sales figures for different products over four quarters:

PRODUCT	Q1	Q2	Q3	Q4
Product A	150	200	250	300
Product B	100	150	200	250
Product C	80	120	160	200

We are able to examine each product's sales trends by looking at this table. For example, we can observe that Product A consistently grows every quarter, whereas Product C grows steadily although initially at a lower rate.

It is crucial to look for differences and similarities between rows and columns when comparing data in tables. This makes it easier to see trends and make decisions based on facts.

To compare the growth of Product A and Product B:
- Product A's increase from Q1 to Q4: 300 - 150 = 150
- Product B's increase from Q1 to Q4: 250 - 100 = 150

Both products have the same total growth over the four quarters, but their starting points and rates of growth differ.

Graph Types and Their Uses
Different types of graphs serve various purposes, each highlighting specific aspects of the data. The most common graph types include bar graphs, line graphs, pie charts, and scatter plots.

- **Bar Graphs:** Bar graphs utilize rectangular bars to depict categorical data, with each bar's length corresponding to the data's value. When comparing several groupings or categories, they are helpful.

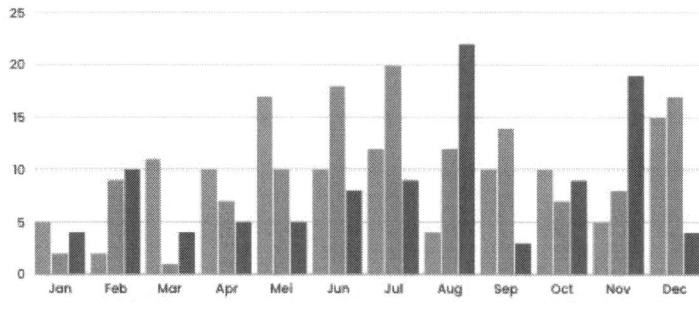

- **Line Graphs:** Data points are shown on line graphs, which illustrate patterns over time by connecting them with straight lines. They are perfect for monitoring data patterns and changes.

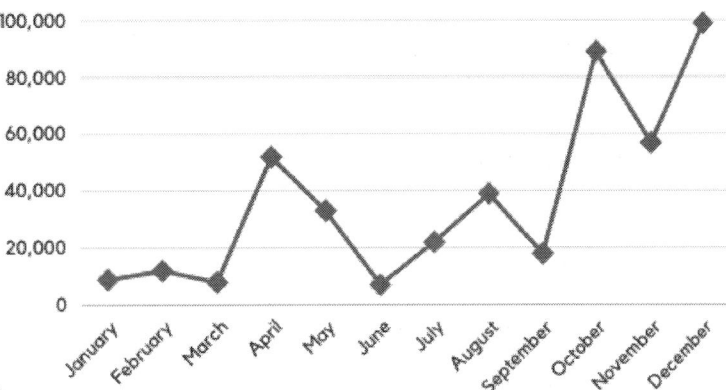

- **Pie Charts:** Pie charts use circles with equal-sized slices to depict data, with each slice representing a particular value. They work well for displaying portions of a larger work.

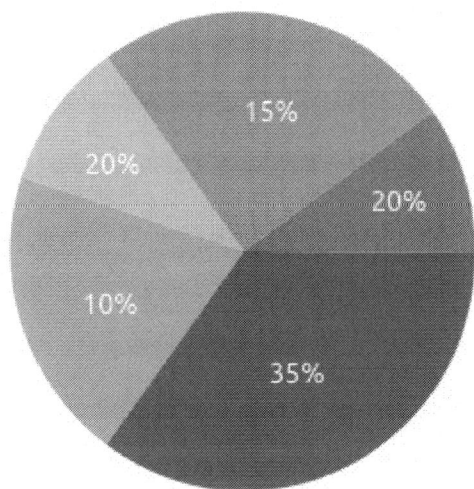

- **Scatter Plots:** The link between two variables is depicted by scatter plots, which show data points on a two-dimensional plane. They are helpful in spotting patterns and relationships.

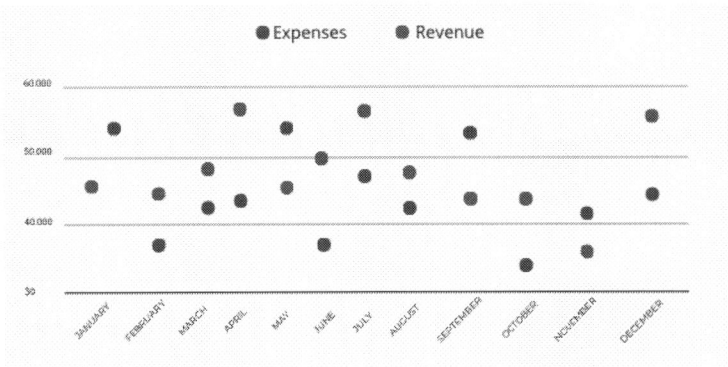

Analyzing Trends and Patterns

For the purpose of forecasting and making wise judgments, data trends and patterns must be found. This involves looking for consistent changes, anomalies, and correlations.

- *Example: Identifying Trends*: A steady upward trend in a line graph displaying monthly sales numbers denotes rising sales, while a downward trend denotes falling sales.

Detecting Anomalies

Data points that substantially depart from the general pattern are called anomalies. Identifying these outliers is important for accurate data analysis.

- *Example: Detecting Anomalies in a Scatter Plot*: In a scatter plot of test scores versus hours studied, a student who studied very little but scored exceptionally high would be an anomaly.

Correlation and Causation

In data analysis, knowing the distinction between causation and correlation is crucial. A correlation suggests a connection between two variables, whereas a causal relationship suggests that one variable influences the other directly.

- *Example: Correlation and Causation*: Although a scatter plot may indicate a relationship between temperature and ice cream sales, this does not imply that temperature variations are caused by ice cream sales. Here, the relationship between temperature and ice cream sales is causative.

Regression Analysis

Regression analysis fits a line or curve to the data points in order to anticipate the relationship between the variables. It is helpful when forecasting future events using past data.

- *Example: Simple Linear Regression*: In a scatter plot of advertising spending versus sales revenue, a regression line can predict future sales based on advertising budgets.

Statistical Significance

Statistical significance determines whether observed patterns in data are likely to be genuine or due to random chance. It is crucial for validating the results of data analysis.

- *Example: Testing Statistical Significance*: When comparing test scores between two groups, statistical tests (e.g., t-tests) determine if the differences are significant or just random variations.

Multi-Variable Comparisons

Analyzing data with multiple variables involves examining the interactions and combined effects of these variables.

- *Example: Multi-Variable Analysis*: A study examining the impact of diet and exercise on weight loss considers both factors simultaneously, providing a more comprehensive analysis.

Mastering the interpretation of tables and graphs is essential for success in the Digital SAT® and various academic and professional fields. Students can effectively examine data, reach precise findings, and make well-informed judgments by honing these skills.

FUNDAMENTAL STATISTICS

Statistics provide tools and techniques for summarizing, evaluating, and deriving conclusions from data sets, which are essential for comprehending and interpreting data. A firm understanding of foundational statistical principles is necessary for success when preparing for the Digital SAT®. Important statistical concepts are covered in this chapter, including measures of variability, measures of central tendency, and the fundamentals of probability.

Statistics is the science concerning with the collection, analysis, arrangement, and interpretation of data. It offers a structure for deliberations grounded in empirical data. The study of statistics includes a variety of methods and resources that aid in identifying trends and connections within data sets.

Measures of Central Tendency

The typical value or center of a data collection is described by measures of central tendency. The median, mean and mode are the most widely used metrics.

- **Mean (Average)**: The sum of the number of data points divided by the whole number of points is the mean. It is the most commonly used measure of central tendency and is calculated using the formula:

$$\text{Mean} = \frac{\sum(\text{Data Points})}{\text{Number of Data Points}}$$

Example: Calculating the Mean
Consider the data set: 5, 7, 3, 8, 10

$$\text{Mean} = \frac{5+7+3+8+10}{5} = \frac{33}{5} = 6.6$$

- **Median**: The median is the middle value of a data set when the values are arranged in ascending order. If the data set has an even number of points, the median is the average of the two middle values.

Example: Calculating the Median
For the data set: 3, 5, 7, 8, 10 (odd number of points)
The median is 7.
For the data set: 3, 5, 7, 8 (even number of points)
The median is $(5 + 7)/2 = 6$.

- **Mode**: The value which appears often in a data set is the mode. If all of the values in a data set are distinct, then there may be one mode, several modes, or no modes at all.

Example: Identifying the Mode
For the data set: 2, 3, 3, 5, 7, 8, 8, 8, 10
The mode is 8.

Measures of Variability

The distribution or dispersion of data points within a data set is described by variability measures. The most common measures are range, variance, and standard deviation.

- **Range**: The largest and lowest values in a data collection are separated by a range. It offers a basic estimation of variability.

Example: Calculating the Range

For the data set: 5, 7, 3, 8, 10
Range = 10 - 3 = 7

- **Variance**: Variance measures the average squared deviation of each data point from the mean. It sheds light on how the data are distributed generally.

Example: Calculating the Variance
For the data set: 5, 7, 3, 8, 10
1. Calculate the mean: 6.6
2. Find the squared deviations from the mean:
    $(5 - 6.6)^2 = 2.56$,
    $(7 - 6.6)^2 = 0.16$,
    $(3 - 6.6)^2 = 12.96$,
    $(8 - 6.6)^2 = 1.96$,
    $(10 - 6.6)^2 = 11.56$
3. Calculate the variance:

$$\text{Variance} = \frac{2.56 + 0.16 + 12.96 + 1.96 + 11.56}{5} = \frac{29.2}{5} = 5.84$$

- **Standard Deviation**: The variance squared is equal to the standard deviation. The average separation between each data point and the mean is given.

Example: Calculating the Standard Deviation
Using the variance calculated above:

$$\text{Standard Deviation} = \sqrt{5.84} \approx 2.42$$

Basics of Probability
Probability is the measure of the likelihood that an event will occur. It ranges from 0 (impossible event) to 1 (certain event). Comprehending probability is a fundamental aspect of analyzing data and forecasting using statistical models. The following formula is used to determine the likelihood of an event:
Probability (P) = Number of Favorable Outcomes/Total Number of Possible Outcomes
Example: Calculating Probability
Rolling a fair six-sided die has the following probability of producing a 4:
$P(4) = 1/6$

Probability Distributions
A random variable's values' probability distribution is explained by probability distributions. Standard probability distributions consist of the normal distribution and the binomial distribution.

- **Binomial Distribution**: The number of successes in a predetermined number of independent Bernoulli trials, each having an equal chance of success, is described by the binomial distribution.

Example: Binomial Distribution
The binomial formula can be used to determine the chance of receiving exactly 3 heads out of 5 coin flips:

$$P(X = k) = \binom{n}{k} p^k (1 - p)^{n-k}$$

where p represents the chance of success on a single trial, k denotes the number of successes, and n represents the number of trials.

- **Normal Distribution**: A continuous, symmetrical probability distribution with a bell-shaped curve around the mean is called a normal distribution. Both the mean (μ) and standard deviation (σ) serve as its descriptive characteristics.

Example: Normal Distribution
A population's adult male heights have a mean of 70 inches and a standard deviation of 3 inches, which corresponds to a normal distribution. The probability of selecting a male at random with a height between 67 and 73 inches can be found using the properties of the normal distribution.

Central Limit Theorem

Regardless of the form of the population distribution, the Central Limit Theorem (CLT) asserts that as sample sizes increase, the distribution of sample means approaches to a normal distribution. A foundational theorem of statistical inference is this one.

Example: Central Limit Theorem

The sample mean distribution will approximate a normal distribution if we repeatedly pick samples of size 30 from a population with any distribution.

Hypothesis Testing

Statistical hypothesis testing is a technique for determining population parameters from sample data. A test statistic is used to assess whether to reject the null hypothesis (H0) once an alternative hypothesis (H1) has been formulated.

Example: Hypothesis Testing

Let's say we wish to determine if a novel medication outperforms the industry norm. We set up hypotheses:

- H0: The new drug doesn't work any better.
- H1: The new drug works better.

After that, in order to draw an inference, we gather sample data and compute a test statistic.

Confidence Intervals

Within a given degree of confidence, a confidence interval is a set of values that most likely contain a population parameter. Both an estimate of the parameter and a reliability indicator are provided.

Example: Confidence Interval

For a sample mean of 50 with a standard deviation of 5 and a sample size of 30, a 95% confidence interval for the population mean can be calculated using the formula:

$$\text{Confidence Interval} = \bar{x} \pm Z \left(\frac{\sigma}{\sqrt{n}} \right)$$

Where:

- $\bar{x}$ is the sample mean (50 in this example)

- Z is the Z-value corresponding to the desired confidence level (1.96 for 95%)

- σ is the standard deviation (5 in this example)

- n is the sample size (30 in this example)

Inserting the values into the formula, we get:

$$\text{Confidence Interval} = 50 \pm 1.96 \left(\frac{5}{\sqrt{30}} \right)$$

CHAPTER 9: SCATTERPLOTS ANALYSIS

BEST FIT LINE

In data analysis, scatterplots are an effective tool that let us see the relationship between two variables. The capacity to create a best fit line, sometimes referred to as a regression line, which aids in summarizing the trend within the data, is one of the most helpful aspects of scatterplots. This chapter examines the idea of the best fit line, including how to calculate it and use it in different situations.

A graph type called a scatterplot shows individual data points according to two variables. Plotted along the two axes that correspond to the variables under study, each point on the scatterplot represents a single observation from a dataset. Finding trends, correlations, and anomalies in the data is made simpler by this graphical depiction.

- *Example: Scatterplot Construction:* Take a look at a dataset that shows how many hours students study and how well they perform on exams. Plotting these data points on a scatterplot with hours studied on the x-axis and exam scores on the y-axis allows us to visually assess the relationship between these two variables.

On a scatterplot, the straight line that most accurately depicts the data is the best fit line, also known as the regression line. By reducing the separation between the line and every data point, it offers the most accurate estimation of the trend present in the data. Y = mx + b is the usual formula for the best fit line, where x is the independent variable, y is the dependent variable, m is the line's slope, and b is the y-intercept.

Calculating the Slope and Intercept

To determine the best fit line, we need to calculate the slope (m) and the y-intercept (b). The intercept shows the value of y when x is zero, but the slope shows the rate of change between the two variables.

Formula for Slope (m):

$$m = \frac{N(\sum xy) - (\sum x)(\sum y)}{N(\sum x^2) - (\sum x)^2}$$

Formula for Y-Intercept (b):

$$b = \frac{(\sum y)(\sum x^2) - (\sum x)(\sum xy)}{N(\sum x^2) - (\sum x)^2}$$

N is the total number of data points, $\sum xy$ represents the sum of the product of every pair of x and y values, $\sum x$ and $\sum y$ denote the sums of the x and y values, respectively, and $\sum x2$ represents the sum of the squares of the x values.

Example Calculation

Let's calculate the best fit line for a small dataset of students' study hours and exam scores:

Hours Studied (x)	Exam Score (y)
2	75
3	80
5	85
7	90

First, calculate the necessary sums:

$$\sum x = 2 + 3 + 5 + 7 + 9 = 26$$

$$\sum y = 75 + 80 + 85 + 90 + 95 = 425$$

$$\sum xy = (2 \cdot 75) + (3 \cdot 80) + (5 \cdot 85) + (7 \cdot 90) + (9 \cdot 95) = 150 + 240 + 425 + 630 + 855 = 2300$$

$$\sum x^2 = 2^2 + 3^2 + 5^2 + 7^2 + 9^2 = 4 + 9 + 25 + 49 + 81 = 168$$

Then, plug these values into the formulas for the slope and intercept:

$$m = \frac{5(2300) - (26)(425)}{5(168) - 26^2} = \frac{11500 - 11050}{840 - 676} = \frac{450}{164} \approx 2.74$$

$$b = \frac{(425)(168) - (26)(2300)}{5(168) - 26^2} = \frac{71400 - 59800}{840 - 676} = \frac{11600}{164} \approx 70.73$$

So, the equation of the best fit line is:

$$y \approx 2.74x + 70.73$$

Plotting the best fit line involves drawing the line that corresponds to the equation (y \approx 2.74x + 70.73) on the scatterplot. The average correlation between the amount of study time and test results is shown by this line.

Interpreting the Best Fit Line

According to the best fit line's slope (2.74), one extra hour of study is linked, on average, to a 2.74-point rise in exam score. The expected exam result for a student who studies 0 hours is shown by the y-intercept (70.73). Numerous real-world uses for the best fit line exist, such as trend analysis, prediction, and comprehending the relationships between variables.

- **Prediction:** One of the primary uses of the best fit line is to make predictions. For instance, by applying the equation y is approximately 2.74x + 70.73, we can forecast the exam result for a student who studies for 6 hours: y is approx 2.74(6) + 70.73 = 16.44 + 70.73 = 87.17. Thus, a student who studies 6 hours is predicted to score approximately 87.17 on the exam.
- **Trend Analysis:** The best fit line facilitates the analysis and identification of data trends. We may determine whether there is a positive, negative, or no relationship between the variables by looking at the slope and direction of the line.
  - *Example: Positive Trend:* The positive slope in the above example suggests a positive correlation between exam results and study hours—that is, when study hours rise, exam scores typically rise as well.

Outliers

Data points classified as outliers are those that substantially depart from the pattern indicated by the best fit line. To comprehend abnormalities and possible inaccuracies in the data, it is crucial to identify outliers.

- *Example: Outlier Identification:* If most students who study 5 hours score around 85, but one student scores 50, that student's score would be considered an outlier.

Correlation Coefficient

Quantifying the strength and direction of a relationship between two variables is done through the use of the correlation coefficient (r). From -1 to 1, it is the range where:

- 1 denotes an ideal positive correlation
- -1 denotes a perfect negative connection
- 0 denotes no correlation

The following formula is used to get the correlation coefficient:

$$r = \frac{N(\sum xy) - (\sum x)(\sum y)}{\sqrt{[N(\sum x^2) - (\sum x)^2][N(\sum y^2) - (\sum y)^2]}}$$

CHAPTER 10: ABSOLUTE VALUE AND NONLINEAR EQUATIONS

UNDERSTANDING ABSOLUTE VALUE

A key idea in mathematics, especially in algebra and calculus, is absolute value. It displays the distance a number has from zero on the number line, regardless of orientation. This chapter explores the properties, uses, and importance of absolute value in a variety of mathematical contexts, delving deeply into the subject. A number x's absolute value is represented by the symbol $|x|$ and has the following definition:

$$\begin{cases} x & \text{if } x \geq 0 \\ -x & \text{if } x < 0 \end{cases}$$

In essence, $|x$ is always non-negative because it measures the magnitude of (x) without regard to its sign. For example:

$|5| = 5$
$|-5| = 5$
$|0| = 0$

Geometric Interpretation

A number's absolute value on the number line indicates how far it is from zero geometrically. This distance is always positive or zero, emphasizing the concept of magnitude irrespective of direction.

- *Example: Geometric Interpretation:* Consider the number line:

$$-\,-\,6\,-\,-\,5\,-\,-\,4\,-\,-\,3\,-\,-\,2\,-\,-\,1\,-\,0\,-\,1\,-\,2\,-\,3\,-\,4\,-\,5\,-\,6\,-$$

The distance of -4 from 0 is 4 units, thus $|-4| = 4$. Similarly, the distance of 4 from 0 is also 4 units, making $|4| = 4$.

Properties of Absolute Value

Absolute value has several key properties that are useful in algebraic manipulations and problem-solving:

1. **Non-negativity:** $|x| \geq 0$ for all x.

2. **Identity:** $|x| = 0$ if and only if $x = 0$.

3. **Multiplicativity:** $|xy| = |x||y|$.

4. **Subadditivity (Triangle Inequality):** $|x + y| \leq |x| + |y|$.

   - *Example: Using Properties:* Consider the numbers x = -3 and y = 4:
- **Non-negativity:** $|-3| = 3$ and $|4| = 4$

- **Multiplicativity:** $|-3 \times 4| = |12| = 12$ and $|-3| \times |4| = 3 \times 4 = 12$

- **Subadditivity:** $|-3 + 4| = |1| = 1$ and $|-3| + |4| = 3 + 4 = 7$, confirming $1 \leq 7$

Absolute Value Equations

Equations involving absolute value often require special consideration due to their piecewise nature. Taking into account various scenarios based on the definition of absolute value is a common step in solving equations involving absolute values.

- *Example: Solving Absolute Value Equations:* Solve the equation $|x - 2| = 5$.

Case 1: $x - 2 \geq 0$ (i.e., $x \geq 2$)

$x - 2 = 5$

$x = 7$

Case 2: $x - 2 < 0$ (i.e., $x < 2$)

$-(x - 2) = 5$

$-x + 2 = 5$

$-x = 3$

$x = -3$

Therefore, the solutions are x = 7 and x = -3.

Inequalities Involving Absolute Value

Solving inequalities involving absolute value often requires breaking them down into separate cases, similar to solving equations.

- *Example: Solving Absolute Value Inequalities:*
  1. Solve the inequality $|x - 3| < 4$. This inequality can be rewritten as two separate inequalities: -4 < x - 3 < 4
  2. Solving these inequalities:

     -4 < x - 3

     x > -1

     x - 3 < 4

     x < 7

     Thus, the solution is: -1 < x < 7

Graphical Interpretation of Inequalities

Graphing absolute value inequalities helps visualize the range of solutions. For $|x - 3| < 4$, the solution set on a number line is the interval (-1, 7).

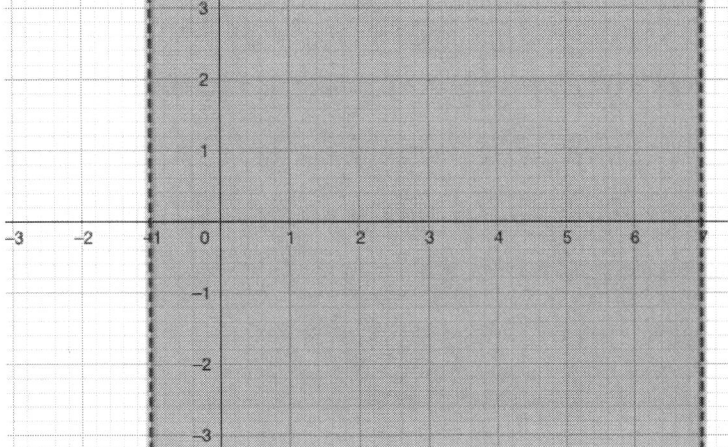

Complex Absolute Value

Complex numbers are included in the scope of absolute value in more complex mathematics. The absolute value of a complex number z = a + bi is defined as:

$$|z| = \sqrt{a^2 + b^2}$$

This definition reflects the distance of the complex number from the origin in the complex plane.

Example: Complex Absolute Value

For the complex number z = 3 + 4i:

$$|z| = \sqrt{3^2 + 4^2} = \sqrt{9 + 16} = \sqrt{25} = 5$$

Solving Absolute Value Equations in Complex Numbers

Consider the equation $|z - (2 + 3i)| = 5$.

This shows a circle with a radius of 5 and a center of 2 + 3i on the complex plane. This circle has any complex number z that satisfies the equation.

Comprehending absolute value is essential for resolving numerous mathematical issues. Its characteristics and uses go beyond basic computations; rather, it is important in both complex mathematical ideas and practical situations. Students who master absolute value will have the necessary skills to flourish in a variety of academic and professional settings, including the Digital SAT®.

EXPLORING NONLINEAR EQUATIONS

Nonlinear equations, which differ from simpler linear equations by incorporating more complex interactions, constitute an important field of study in mathematics. On a graph, nonlinear equations produce curves rather than straight lines, which complicates both their analysis and solutions. This chapter explores the properties, methods, and uses of nonlinear equations, providing a thorough grasp that is necessary to succeed on the Digital SAT®.

Equations that incorporate products of variables or elevate the variables to a power other than one are referred to as nonlinear equations. Although a nonlinear equation's basic structure can vary greatly, it frequently contains terms like (x^2), (xy), higher-order polynomials, and transcendental functions like logarithmic, exponential, and trigonometric functions.

Types of Nonlinear Equations

- Quadratic Equations: $ax^2 + bx + c = 0$
- Cubic Equations: $ax^3 + bx^2 + cx + d = 0$
- Exponential Equations: $a \cdot e^{bx} = c$
- Logarithmic Equations: $a \cdot \log_b(x) = c$
- Trigonometric Equations: $a \cdot \sin(bx) = c$

Solving Quadratic Equations

Among the nonlinear equations that appear on the SAT® the most frequently are quadratic equations. A quadratic equation has the conventional form $ax^2 + bx + c = 0$.

Quadratic equations can be solved in a number of ways, including factoring, completing the square, and using the quadratic formula.

Example: Solving by Factoring

Consider the quadratic equation: $x^2 - 5x + 6 = 0$

To factor: $(x - 2)(x - 3) = 0$

The solutions are obtained by setting each element to zero: [x = 2] [x = 3]

Using the Quadratic Formula

Any quadratic problem with the formula $ax^2 + bx + c = 0$ can have its solutions discovered by applying the quadratic formula:

$$x = \frac{-b \pm \sqrt{b^2 - 4ac}}{2a}$$

Example: Solve $2x^2 - 4x - 6 = 0$ using the quadratic formula.
Here, a = 2, b = -4, and c = -6.

$$x = \frac{-(-4)\pm\sqrt{(-4)^2-4\cdot2\cdot(-6)}}{2\cdot2}$$

$$x = \frac{4\pm\sqrt{16+48}}{4}$$

$$x = \frac{4\pm\sqrt{64}}{4}$$

$$x = \frac{4\pm8}{4}$$

Thus, the solutions are: [x = 3] [x = -1]

Graphical Solutions to Nonlinear Equations

Using a graph to solve nonlinear equations visually is quite helpful when trying to comprehend how these functions behave. A parabola, for example, represents the graph of the quadratic equation y = ax^2 + bx + c. The equation's solutions are found at the spots where the parabola crosses the x-axis.

Solving Nonlinear Systems of Equations

In some cases, nonlinear equations are part of a system of equations. Finding the values of the variables that concurrently satisfy each equation is the first step in solving complex problems.

Example: Nonlinear System

Consider the system: [y = x² + 3] [y = 2x + 1]

To solve this system, set the equations equal to each other: [x² + 3 = 2x + 1] [x² - 2x + 2 = 0]

Solve using the quadratic formula

$$x = \frac{-(-2)\pm\sqrt{(-2)^2-4\cdot1\cdot2}}{2\cdot1}$$

$$x = \frac{2\pm\sqrt{4-8}}{2}$$

$$x = \frac{2\pm\sqrt{-4}}{2}$$

$$x = \frac{2\pm2i}{2}$$

$$x = 1\pm i$$

Thus, the solutions are x = 1 + i and x = 1 - i, indicating complex solutions.

Analyzing Nonlinear Inequalities

Expressions with raised variables to powers other than one are known as nonlinear inequalities. Solving these inequalities requires understanding the behavior of the functions involved and identifying the intervals where the inequality holds true.

Example: Solving Nonlinear Inequality

Solve x² - 4x + 3 < 0.

First, factor the quadratic expression: (x - 1)(x - 3) < 0

Determine the intervals by solving the equation (x - 1)(x - 3) = 0, which gives x = 1 and x = 3. These values divide the number line into intervals:

$$(-\infty, 1), \ (1, 3), \text{ and } (3, \infty)$$

Test a point within each interval:

- For $x = 0$ in $(-\infty, 1)$: $(0 - 1)(0 - 3) = 3$ (not less than 0)

- For $x = 2$ in $(1, 3)$: $(2 - 1)(2 - 3) = -1$ (less than 0)

- For $x = 4$ in $(3, \infty)$: $(4 - 1)(4 - 3) = 3$ (not less than 0)

Thus, the solution to the inequality is 1 < x < 3.

Nonlinear Differential Equations

Nonlinear differential equations involve derivatives of nonlinear functions. Advanced mathematical modeling often involves these equations, especially in disciplines like engineering and physics.

Example: Nonlinear Differential Equation

Consider the nonlinear differential equation: $dy/dx = y^2 - x$

Solving such equations often requires specialized techniques, such as separation of variables or numerical methods, due to their complexity.

Numerical Solutions

Numerical approaches are required in numerous practical cases where analytical solutions are not possible for nonlinear equations. Techniques such as the Newton-Raphson method provide iterative solutions to approximate the roots of nonlinear equations.

Example: Newton-Raphson Method

To solve $f(x) = 0$ using the Newton-Raphson method, iterate using:

$$x_{n+1} = x_n - \frac{f(x_n)}{f'(x_n)}$$

For the equation $x^3 - x - 2 = 0$, start with an initial guess x_0, and iterate until convergence.

CHAPTER 11: EXPONENTS, RADICALS, POLYNOMIALS, AND RATIONAL EXPRESSIONS

EXPONENTS

Exponents, which show the repeated multiplication of a base number, are essential concepts in mathematics. They are fundamental to many algebraic formulas and are necessary to comprehend more complex mathematical concepts. In order to give students a comprehensive preparation for the Digital SAT®, this chapter examines the fundamentals of exponents, their characteristics, and their applications in a variety of mathematical contexts.

The multiplicity of a number, referred to as the base, by itself is shown by an exponent. It appears as a tiny number to the base's upper right. For instance, the expression a^n, which represents a multiplied by itself n times, has a for the base and a for the exponent.

$a^n = a \times a \times a \times a \dots \times a$ (n times)

Properties of Exponents

It is essential to comprehend exponent properties in order to simplify expressions and solve equations involving exponents. The key properties include:

1. **Product of Powers Property:** $a^m \times a^n = a^{m+n}$. This principle says that you add the exponents when multiplying two equations with the same base.
2. **Quotient of Powers Property:** $a^m/a^n = a^{m-n}$. You deduct the exponent in the numerator from the exponent in the denominator when dividing two expressions with the same base.
3. **Power of a Power Property:** $(a^m)^n = a^{m \times n}$. Exponents are multiplied when raising one to a higher exponent.
4. **Power of a Product Property:** $(ab)^n = a^n \times b^n$. This property allows you to distribute the exponent to each factor within the parentheses.
5. **Power of a Quotient Property:** $\left(\frac{a}{b}\right)^n = \frac{a^n}{b^n}$. You can allocate the exponent to the denominator and the numerator thanks to this characteristic.
6. **Zero Exponent Property:** $a^0 = 1$. Raised to the power of zero, any non-zero base equals one.
7. **Negative Exponent Property:** $a^{-n} = \frac{1}{a^n}$. When the base is elevated to the positive exponent, the reciprocal is represented by a negative exponent.

Examples and Applications

Example 1: Simplifying Exponential Expressions
Simplify the expression $2^3 \times 2^4$.
Using the Product of Powers Property: $2^3 \times 2^4 = 2^{3+4} = 2^7$
Example 2: Applying the Quotient of Powers Property

Simplify the expression $\frac{5^6}{5^2}$.

Using the Quotient of Powers Property: $\frac{5^6}{5^2} = 5^{6-2} = 5^4$

Example 3: Power of a Power
Simplify the expression $(3^2)^3$.
Using the Power of a Power Property: $(3^2)^3 = 3^{2 \times 3} = 3^6$

Exponential Growth and Decay

Exponents play a critical role in modeling exponential growth and decay, common in fields like biology, finance, and physics.
Exponential Growth Exponential growth can be described by the formula: $P(t) = P_0 e^{rt}$

Where:
- P(t) is the amount of something at time t.
- P_0 is the starting amount.
- r stands for growth rate.
- e is the natural logarithm's base, roughly equal to 2.71828.

Example: Population Growth: A population of bacteria doubles every hour. If the initial population is 100 bacteria, the population after (t) hours is given by: $P(t) = 100 \times 2^t$

Exponential Decay
Exponential decay follows a similar model but with a negative growth rate: $P(t) = P_0 e^{-rt}$
Example: Radioactive Decay: The amount of a radioactive substance decreases over time according to its half-life. If a substance has a half-life of 5 years, the remaining amount after t years is:

$$P(t) = P_0 \left(\frac{1}{2}\right)^{\frac{t}{5}}$$

RADICALS

An essential component of algebra and advanced mathematics is radicals. These are expressions using roots, cube roots and higher-order roots with the most popular ones being square roots. To succeed on the Digital SAT® and in many other mathematical issues, one must have a solid understanding of radicals. This chapter explores the basic ideas, characteristics, and uses of radicals, offering a comprehensive overview of this significant subject.
A radicand, or the number or expression inside the root, and the root sign, $\sqrt{\ }$, are both parts of a radical expression. Although cube roots $\sqrt[3]{\ }$ and higher-order roots exist, the square root is the most often occurring radical.

$\sqrt{a}$ (Square Root)

$\sqrt[3]{a}$ (Cube Root)

$\sqrt[n]{a}$ (n-th Root)

Properties of Radicals

1. **Product Property of Radicals:** $\sqrt{a} \times \sqrt{b} = \sqrt{a \times b}$. This property allows you to multiply the radicands before taking the root.

2. **Quotient Property of Radicals:** $\sqrt{\frac{a}{b}} = \frac{\sqrt{a}}{\sqrt{b}}$. This property allows you to divide the radicands before taking the root.

3. **Simplifying Radicals:** To Utilize the properties of radicals, factor the radicand into its prime factors, and simplify radical expressions. For example: $\sqrt{72} = \sqrt{36 \times 2} = \sqrt{36} \times \sqrt{2} = 6\sqrt{2}$

4. **Adding and Subtracting Radicals:** Radicals can be added or subtracted only if they have the same radicand. For instance: $3\sqrt{2} + 2\sqrt{2} = 5\sqrt{2}$

5. **Rationalizing the Denominator:** When a radical appears in the denominator, it is often helpful to eliminate it by multiplying the numerator and the denominator by a suitable radical: $\frac{1}{\sqrt{2}} \times \frac{\sqrt{2}}{\sqrt{2}} = \frac{\sqrt{2}}{2}$

Examples and Applications

Example 1: Simplifying Radical Expressions

Simplify $\sqrt{50}$

First, factor 50 into prime factors:

$$50 = 25 \times 2 = 5^2 \times 2$$

Then, apply the product property of radicals:

$$\sqrt{50} = \sqrt{5^2 \times 2} = 5\sqrt{2}$$

Example 2: Adding and Subtracting Radicals

Simplify $3\sqrt{18} - 2\sqrt{8} + \sqrt{50}$.

First, simplify each radical:

$$3\sqrt{18} = 3 \times 3\sqrt{2} = 9\sqrt{2}$$
$$2\sqrt{8} = 2 \times 2\sqrt{2} = 4\sqrt{2}$$
$$\sqrt{50} = 5\sqrt{2}$$

Then, combine the like terms:

$$9\sqrt{2} - 4\sqrt{2} + 5\sqrt{2} = (9 - 4 + 5)\sqrt{2} = 10\sqrt{2}$$

Example 3: Rationalizing the Denominator

Simplify $\frac{3}{2\sqrt{5}}$.

Multiply the numerator and the denominator by $\sqrt{5}$

$$\frac{3}{2\sqrt{5}} \times \frac{\sqrt{5}}{\sqrt{5}} = \frac{3\sqrt{5}}{2 \times 5} = \frac{3\sqrt{5}}{10}$$

Operations with Radicals

Radicals can be involved in various operations, including multiplication, division, addition, and subtraction, each following specific rules and properties.

Multiplication of Radicals

When multiplying radicals, multiply the radicands together: $\sqrt{a} \times \sqrt{b} = \sqrt{a \times b}$

Example: $\sqrt{3} \times \sqrt{12} = \sqrt{3 \times 12} = \sqrt{36} = 6$

Division of Radicals

When dividing radicals, divide the radicands: $\frac{\sqrt{a}}{\sqrt{b}} = \sqrt{\frac{a}{b}}$

Example: $\frac{\sqrt{18}}{\sqrt{2}} = \sqrt{\frac{18}{2}} = \sqrt{9} = 3$

Higher-Order Radicals

Higher-order radicals follow the same properties as square roots but involve different root indices.

Example: Simplifying Cube Roots

Simplify $\sqrt[3]{54}$.

First, factor 54 into prime factors: $54 = 27 \times 2 = 3^3 \times 2$

Then, apply the properties of cube roots: $\sqrt[3]{54} = \sqrt[3]{3^3 \times 2} = 3\sqrt[3]{2}$

Common Mistakes and Misconceptions
1. **Incorrect Simplification**: Students may incorrectly simplify radicals, such as failing to properly factor the radicand or incorrectly applying properties.
2. **Combining Unlike Radicals**: Adding or subtracting radicals with different radicands is a common mistake.
3. **Forgetting to Rationalize**: Leaving radicals in the denominator is another frequent error.

POLINOMIALS

The fundamental building blocks of algebra, polynomials have application in a wide range of mathematical fields. In order to provide readers with the thorough understanding required to grasp polynomials on the Digital SAT®, this chapter examines the fundamental ideas, operations, and applications of polynomials.

A polynomial is an algebraic statement with variables (sometimes called indeterminates) and coefficients that only needs the non-negative integer exponents of variables to be added, subtracted, multiplied, and divided.

A general form of a polynomial in one variable x is expressed as: $P(x) = a_n x_n + a_{n-1} x^{n-1} + \ldots + a_1 x + a_0$ where (a_n, a_{n-1}, $\ldots$, a_1, a_0) are coefficients, x is the variable, and n is a non-negative integer representing the degree of the polynomial. The degree of the polynomial is the greatest power of the variable in the polynomial.

Types of Polynomials
- **Monomial**: A polynomial with a single term. Example: $5x^3$
- **Binomial**: A polynomial with exactly two terms. Example: $3x^2 + 2x$
- **Trinomial**: A polynomial with exactly three terms. Example: $x^2 - 4x + 4$

Operations on Polynomials
Polynomials can undergo various operations, including addition, subtraction, multiplication, and division. Understanding these operations is essential for solving polynomial-related problems effectively.

Addition and Subtraction of Polynomials
To add or subtract polynomials, combine like terms, which are terms that have the same variable raised to the same power.
- *Example: Addition:* Add $3x^2 + 2x + 1$ and $2x^2 - x + 3$: $(3x^2 + 2x + 1) + (2x^2 - x + 3) = 3x^2 + 2x^2 + 2x - x + 1 + 3 = 5x^2 + x + 4$
- *Example: Subtraction:* Subtract $2x^2 - x + 3$ from $3x^2 + 2x + 1$: $(3x^2 + 2x + 1) - (2x^2 - x + 3) = 3x^2 - 2x^2 + 2x + x + 1 - 3 = x + 3x - 2$

Multiplication of Polynomials
Utilizing the distributive property, which is sometimes referred to as the FOIL approach for binomials, allows you to multiply polynomials by combining like terms after multiplying each term in the first polynomial by each term in the second polynomial.
- *Example: Multiplication:* Multiply $(x + 2)(x + 3)$: $(x + 2)(x + 3) = x(x + 3) + 2(x + 3) = x^2 + 3x + 2x + 6 = x^2 + 5x + 6$

Division of Polynomials
Polynomials can be divided using long division or synthetic division. While long division is more versatile and may be applied to any polynomial, synthetic division is a straightforward method that can only be utilized when dividing by a linear polynomial.
- *Example: Long Division:* Divide $x^3 + 2x^2 + 4x + 3$ by $x + 1$:
  The dividend's first term is divided by the divisor's first term: $x^3/x = x^2$
  Multiply the entire divisor by this quotient: $x^2(x + 1) = x^3 + x^2$
  Subtract the result from the original polynomial: $(x^3 + 2x^2 + 4x + 3) - (x^3 + x^2) = x^2 + 4x + 3$
  Repeat the process with the new polynomial: $x^2 + 4x + 3$

Factoring Polynomials

The process of factoring polynomials entails representing a polynomial as the sum of its simpler counterparts. In order to simplify expressions and solve polynomial equations, this procedure is necessary.

- *Example: Factoring*: Quadratic Polynomials Factor $x^2 + 5x + 6$:
  Locate two integers that sum up to the linear coefficient (5) and multiply to the constant term 6: 2 and 3.
  The polynomial can be rewritten as the product of two binomials: $x^2 + 5x + 6 = (x + 2)(x + 3)$.

Graphing Polynomials

Plotting points on a coordinate plane allows one to see the behavior of a polynomial through graphing. A polynomial function of degree n will have n roots (real or complex), and at most n-1 turning points on its graph.

Steps to Graph Polynomials

- **Determine the End Behavior**: The leading term, $a_n x_n$, determines how a polynomial function behaves in the end. If n is even, both ends of the graph will move in the same direction (either up or down). If n is odd, the ends will move in opposite directions.
- **Find the Zeros**: The values of x for which $P(x) = 0$ are known as the polynomial's Zeros, or roots. These are the locations on the graph where the x-axis is crossed.
- **Plot Additional Points**: Choose values of x around the zeros and calculate the corresponding y values to get more points to plot.
- **Sketch the Graph**: Make sure the graph passes through the zeros and exhibits the final behavior by connecting the points with a smooth curve.

Example: Graphing a Quadratic Polynomial
Graph $P(x) - x^2 - 4x + 3$:

- Determine the end behavior: The leading term is x^2, so both ends move up.
- Find the zeros: $x^2 - 4x + 3 = 0$ factors to $(x - 1)(x - 3) = 0$, so the zeros are $x = 1$ and $x = 3$.
- Plot additional points: Calculate P(0), P(2), and P(4) : [P(0) = 3] [P(2) = -1] [P(4) = 3]
- Using these points and the zeros, sketch out the graph.

Common Mistakes and Misconceptions

- **Incorrectly Combining Like Terms**: Make sure you combine terms only when their exponents and variables are the same.
- **Errors in Distribution**: Carefully apply the distributive property when multiplying polynomials to avoid missing terms.
- **Factoring Errors**: Always check factored forms by expanding them to verify correctness.

RATIONAL EXPRESSIONS AND EQUATIONS

Both the SAT® and general mathematical proficiency depend on rational expressions and equations, which are fundamental elements of the mathematical landscape. They blend the intricacy of fractions with the algebraic concepts, necessitating a sophisticated grasp of manipulation, simplification, and problem-solving techniques.

A fraction is referred to as a rational expression when the numerator and/or denominator are polynomials. For example:

$$\frac{2x+3}{x^2-4}$$

Similar to numerical fractions, rational expressions can also be made simpler. To do this, factor the polynomials in both the denominator and the numerator, eliminating any common factors.

Simplifying Rational Expressions

Take these actions to simplify a rational expression:

1. **Factor the Numerator and Denominator**: Break down both the numerator and the denominator into their component factors.
2. **Cancel Common Factors**: Identify and cancel out any common factors that appear in both the numerator and the denominator.

Example 1:
Reduce the rational expression to:

$$\frac{6x^2-12x}{3x}$$

Factor the denominator as well as the numerator:

$$\frac{6x(x-2)}{3x}$$

Cancel the common factor of (3x):

$$\frac{6x(x-2)}{3x} = \frac{2(x-2)}{1} = 2(x-2)$$

Example 2:
Reduce the rational expression to:

$$\frac{x^2-9}{x^2-x-6}$$

Factor the denominator as well as the numerator:

$$\frac{(x+3)(x-3)}{(x-3)(x+2)}$$

Cancel the common factor of (x - 3):

$$\frac{(x+3)(x-3)}{(x-3)(x+2)} = \frac{x+3}{x+2}$$

Operations with Rational Expressions

Just as with numerical fractions, we can perform addition, subtraction, division and multiplication, with rational expressions.

Multiplication and Division:

For multiplication and division, factor all expressions fully and cancel common factors before performing the operation.
Example: Multiply the rational expressions:

$$\frac{2x}{3} \cdot \frac{9}{4x}$$

Factor (if necessary) and multiply:

$$\frac{2x \cdot 9}{3 \cdot 4x} = \frac{18x}{12x}$$

Cancel common factors:

$$\frac{18x}{12x} = \frac{3}{2}$$

Addition and Subtraction:

Find a common denominator for rational expressions before combining the numerators over it to add or subtract.

Example: Add the rational expressions:

$$\frac{3}{x-2} + \frac{4}{x+3}$$

Find a common denominator: $(x - 2)(x + 3)$

Rewrite each fraction with the common denominator:

$$\frac{3(x+3)}{(x-2)(x+3)} + \frac{4(x-2)}{(x-2)(x+3)}$$

Combine the numerators:

$$\frac{3(x+3)+4(x-2)}{(x-2)(x+3)} = \frac{3x+9+4x-8}{(x-2)(x+3)} = \frac{7x+1}{(x-2)(x+3)}$$

Complex Fractions

Complex fractions contain fractions within fractions. Clearing the inner denominators by multiplying the numerator and denominator by a common factor is necessary to simplify these.

Example: Simplify the complex fraction:

$$\frac{\frac{2}{x}+\frac{3}{y}}{\frac{4}{x^2}-\frac{9}{y^2}}$$

Simplify the numerator and the denominator separately:

Numerator:

$$\frac{2}{x} + \frac{3}{y} = \frac{2y+3x}{xy}$$

Denominator:

$$\frac{4}{x^2} - \frac{9}{y^2} = \frac{4y^2-9x^2}{x^2y^2} = \frac{(2y+3x)(2y-3x)}{x^2y^2}$$

Combine the simplified forms:

$$\frac{\frac{2y+3x}{xy}}{\frac{(2y+3x)(2y-3x)}{x^2y^2}}$$

Simplify by multiplying by the reciprocal of the denominator:

$$\frac{2y+3x}{xy} \cdot \frac{x^2y^2}{(2y+3x)(2y-3x)} = \frac{xy(2y+3x)}{xy(2y+3x)(2y-3x)} = \frac{1}{2y-3x}$$

Solving Rational Equations

Rational equations involve rational expressions set equal to each other. By multiplying by a common multiple of all the denominators, one can eliminate the denominators and solve them.

Example: Solve the rational equation:

$$\frac{2}{x} + 3 = \frac{4}{x+1}$$

Find a common denominator and multiply through:

2(x + 1) + 3x(x + 1) = 4x

Simplify and solve the resulting equation:

$2x + 2 + 3x^2 + 3x = 4x$

$3x^2 + x + 2 = 0$

Solve the quadratic equation using the quadratic formula:

$$x = \frac{-b \pm \sqrt{b^2 - 4ac}}{2a}$$

Here, a = 3, b = 1, and c = 2:

$$x = \frac{-1 \pm \sqrt{1 - 24}}{6}$$

Since the discriminant is negative, this equation has no real solutions.

Applications of Rational Equations

Rational equations often model real-world scenarios involving rates, such as work problems, motion problems, and mixture problems.

Example: Two workers, A and B, can complete a task in 5 and 3 hours, respectively. In what amount of time will they need to collaborate to finish the assignment?

Let t be the amount of hours needed for them to finish the assignment together.

Worker A's rate: 1/5 tasks per hour. Worker B's rate: 1/3 tasks per hour.

Combined rate equation:

1/5 + 1/3 = 1/t

Find a common denominator and solve for (t):

$$\frac{3+5}{15} = \frac{1}{t}$$

$$\frac{8}{15} = \frac{1}{t}$$

$$t = \frac{15}{8} \approx 1.875 \text{ hours}$$

Graphing Rational Functions

Finding intercepts, holes in the graph, and vertical and horizontal asymptotes are all part of graphing rational functions.

Steps to Graph a Rational Function:

- **Find Vertical Asymptotes**: After setting the denominator to zero, find x.
- **Find Horizontal Asymptotes**: Examine and contrast the degrees of the denominator and numerator.
  - In the event that the denominator's degree is greater than the numerator's, y = 0 represents the horizontal asymptote.
  - The horizontal asymptote, where a and b are the leading coefficients, is y = a/b if the degrees are equal.
- **Find Intercepts**: Set x = 0 for the y-intercept and set the numerator equal to zero for the x-intercepts.
- **Identify Holes**: If there are common factors in the numerator and denominator, the function has holes at those x values.
- **Plot Points**: To comprehend the graph's behavior, plot a number of points around the asymptotes.

CHAPTER 12: QUADRATIC FUNCTIONS

FACTORING QUADRATIC EQUATIONS

An essential algebraic core ability for the Digital SAT® is factoring quadratic equations. This chapter explores factoring techniques and ideas in detail, providing a thorough examination of approaches and real-world applications. Any equation with the following form is a quadratic equation:

$ax^2 + bx + c = 0$

where $a \neq 0$ and a, b, and c are constants. Rewriting the quadratic formula as a product of two binomials is the process of factoring.

Basic Factoring Technique

The simplest form of factoring is applied when $a = 1$. Consider the quadratic equation:

$x^2 + 5x + 6 = 0$

We must identify two numbers that add up to b (5) and multiply to c (6) in order to factor this. These numbers are 2 and 3. Thus, the factored form is:

$(x + 2)(x + 3) = 0$

Setting each factor equal to zero gives the solutions:

$$x + 2 = 0 \implies x = -2$$
$$x + 3 = 0 \implies x = -3$$

Factoring with a ≠ 1

When $a \neq 1$, the process involves a few more steps. Consider the quadratic equation:

$2x^2 + 7x + 3 = 0$

Multiply a and c: $2 \cdot 3 = 6$

1. Determine which two numbers sum up to 7 and multiply by 6: 6 and 1 are these numbers.
2. Rewrite the middle term using these numbers: $2x^2 + 6x + x + 3 = 0$
3. Factor by grouping: $2x(x + 3) + 1(x + 3) = 0$
4. Factor out the common binomial: $(2x + 1)(x + 3) = 0$
5. Solve each factor:

$$2x + 1 = 0 \implies x = -\frac{1}{2}$$
$$x + 3 = 0 \implies x = -3$$

Special Cases in Factoring Quadratics

1. Perfect Square Trinomials: A trinomial that factors into the square of a binomial is called a perfect square. For example:

$x^2 + 6x + 9 = (x + 3)^2$

To identify a perfect square trinomial:

- Verify that the last term and the initial term are perfect squares.
- Verify whether the square roots of the first and last terms multiply the middle term by twice.

2. Difference of Squares: A difference of squares can be factored into the product of two conjugates:

$a^2 - b^2 = (a + b)(a - b)$

For example:

$x^2 - 16 = (x + 4)(x - 4)$

3. Sum and Difference of Cubes: While not a quadratic, understanding the factorization of cubes can sometimes aid in recognizing patterns:

$a^3 + b^3 = (a + b)(a^2 - ab + b^2)$
$a^3 - b^3 = (a - b)(a^2 + ab + b^2)$

Complex Quadratic Equations

When quadratics involve higher powers or multiple variables, they can often be reduced to a simpler form through substitution.

Example:

Factor the quadratic in terms of y:

$4x^4 + 4x^2y + y^2$

1. Substitute $u = x^2$:
   $4u^2 + 4uy + y^2$
2. Factor the resulting quadratic: $(2u + y)^2$
3. Substitute back $u = x^2$:
   $(2x^2 + y)^2$

Factoring by Completing the Square

Completing the square is a method that can be used to factor quadratics, especially when solving quadratic equations. Using this technique, a quadratic expression is converted into a perfect square trinomial.

Steps:

1. **Rewrite the quadratic:**

$$ax^2 + bx + c \rightarrow x^2 + bx + \left(\frac{b}{2}\right)^2 - \left(\frac{b}{2}\right)^2 + c$$

2. **Form the perfect square trinomial:**

$$x^2 + bx + \left(\frac{b}{2}\right)^2$$

3. **Subtract the added term and simplify:**

$$\left(x + \frac{b}{2}\right)^2 - \left(\frac{b}{2}\right)^2 + c$$

Example:

Complete the square for the quadratic equation:

$x^2 + 6x + 8 = 0$

1. **Rewrite the middle term:**
   $x^2 + 6x + 9 - 9 + 8 = 0$
   $(x + 3)^2 - 1 = 0$
2. **Solve the equation:**

$$(x + 3)^2 = 1$$
$$x + 3 = \pm 1$$
$$x = -3 \pm 1$$

Quadratic Formula

Although factoring is frequently the best approach, it isn't always feasible to solve quadratic problems. The quadratic formula is a dependable substitute in certain circumstances. The quadratic formula, which may be used to solve any quadratic equation, is produced via the procedure of completing the square.

$$x = \frac{-b \pm \sqrt{b^2 - 4ac}}{2a}$$

Example:

Utilizing the quadratic formula, solve the quadratic equation:

$3x^2 - 5x + 2 = 0$

1. **Identify a, b, and c:**
   $a = 3, b = -5, c = 2$

2. **Substitute into the quadratic formula:**

$$x = \frac{-(-5) \pm \sqrt{(-5)^2 - 4(3)(2)}}{2(3)}$$

3. **Simplify the expression:**

$$x = \frac{5 \pm \sqrt{25 - 24}}{6}$$

$$x = \frac{5 \pm \sqrt{1}}{6}$$

$$x = \frac{5 \pm 1}{6}$$

4. **Solve for x:**

x = 1 or x = 2/3

Real-World Applications

Factoring quadratic equations is useful in a variety of domains, including biology, physics, engineering, and economics. It's not only an intellectual exercise. Under some circumstances, quadratics can also be used to describe population expansion and optimize functions such as projectile motion.

Example in Physics:

In projectile motion, the height h of an object at any time t can be modeled by a quadratic equation:

$h(t) = -16t^2 + vt + h_0$

where v is the initial velocity, and h_0 is the initial height. It is possible to calculate the moment the projectile strikes the ground ($h(t) = 0$) by factoring this equation.

Example in Economics:

In economics, the profit P can be modeled as a quadratic equation in terms of the number of units x sold:

$P(x) = ax^2 + bx + c$

Factoring this equation can help determine the break-even points and the number of units that maximize profit.

GRAPHINNG QUADRATIC FUNCTIONS

For both algebraic proficiency and success on the Digital SAT®, graphing quadratic functions is a necessary skill. When quadratic functions are graphed, they produce parabolas, as shown by the equation y = ax2 + bx + c. Visualizing quadratic equation answers and analyzing real-world data are made easier by knowing how to graph these functions. A symmetrical curve that opens either upwards or downwards is called a parabola, and it is formed by a quadratic function. The quadratic equation can be expressed generally as:

y = ax2 + bx + c

Here, a, b, and c are constants, and a ≠ 0. The sign of a determines the direction of the parabola:

- If a > 0, the parabola opens upwards.
- If a < 0, the parabola opens downwards.

Depending on the way the parabola opens, the vertex is either its highest or lowest point. A vertical line known as the axis of symmetry splits the parabola in half, creating mirror images of each other.

Vertex Form of a Quadratic Function

A quadratic function can also be expressed in vertex form:

y = a(x - h)2 + k

where (h, k) is the vertex of the parabola. This form is particularly useful for graphing because it directly provides the vertex's coordinates and makes it easier to see how the graph shifts and stretches.

Finding the Vertex

To find the vertex of a quadratic function in standard form, use the following formulas:

$$h = -\frac{b}{2a}$$

$$k = f(h) = a\left(-\frac{b}{2a}\right)^2 + b\left(-\frac{b}{2a}\right) + c$$

Example:

Find the vertex of the quadratic function $y = 2x^2 - 4x + 1$.

1. Calculate h:

$$h = -\frac{-4}{2(2)} = 1$$

2. Calculate (k):

$$k = 2(1)^2 - 4(1) + 1 = 2 - 4 + 1 = -1$$

The vertex is (1, -1).

Graphing Step-by-Step

1. **Identify the direction of the parabola:** Determine whether it opens upwards or downwards by the sign of a.
2. **Find the vertex:** Use the formulas above to find the coordinates (h, k).
3. **Determine the axis of symmetry:** The line x = h is the axis of symmetry.
4. **Find the y-intercept:** Set x = 0 and solve for y. This gives the point (0, c).
5. **Plot additional points:** Choose values for x around the vertex and solve for y to get more points on the graph.
6. **Draw the parabola:** Plot all points, draw the axis of symmetry, and sketch the parabola.

Example:

1. Graph the quadratic function $y = -x^2 + 2x + 3$.
   Since a = -1, the parabola widens downward.
2. Find the vertex:

$$h = -\frac{2}{2(-1)} = 1$$

$$k = -1(1)^2 + 2(1) + 3 = -1 + 2 + 3 = 4$$

   The vertex is (1, 4).
3. The axis of symmetry is x = 1.
4. Find the y-intercept:
   $y = -0^2 + 2(0) + 3 = 3$
   The y-intercept is (0, 3).
5. Plot additional points by choosing x values around 1 (e.g., 0, 2).
   For (x = 0):
   $y = -0^2 + 2(0) + 3 = 3$
   For (x = 2):
   $y = -(2)^2 + 2(2) + 3 = -4 + 4 + 3 = 3$
   Points are (0, 3) and (2, 3).
   Plot all points: (1, 4), (0, 3), (2, 3), and sketch the parabola opening downwards.

Transformations of Quadratic Functions

Quadratic functions can undergo various transformations that affect their graphs. These include vertical shifts, horizontal shifts, reflections, and stretches or compressions.

1. **Vertical Shifts:** The graph of $(y = ax^2 + bx + c)$ shifts vertically when a constant is added or subtracted. When $y = ax^2 + bx + c + k$ is used, for instance, the graph is shifted up by k units for k > 0 and down by k units for k < 0.

2. **Horizontal Shifts**: The graph shifts horizontally when the x-variable is replaced by (x - h). For instance, the graph is shifted by h units if h > 0 and by h units if h < 0 when $y = a(x - h)^2 + k$ is applied.

3. **Reflections**: The graph reflects over the x-axis when a is negative. For instance, $y = -ax^2 + bx + c$ reflects the graph of $y = ax^2 + bx + c$ over the x-axis.

4. **Stretches and Compressions**: The graph stretches vertically if $|a| > 1$ and compresses if $|a| < 1$. For example, $y = 2x^2$ stretches the graph of $y = x^2$, making it narrower, while $y = \frac{1}{2}x^2$) compresses it, making it wider.

Example:

Consider the function $y = 3(x - 2)^2 - 4$. Analyze its transformations.

- **Horizontal Shift**: The function shifts right by 2 units.
- **Vertical Shift**: The function shifts down by 4 units.
- **Vertical Stretch**: A factor of 3 is applied to stretch the graph.

These modifications are visible in the vertex form, which facilitates graph sketching.

CHAPTER 13: GEOMETRY AND TRIGONOMETRY CONCEPTS

LINES AND ANGLES

A fundamental component of the mathematics curriculum, geometry provides vital instruments for comprehending the material world. Many geometric concepts are based on lines and angles, thus it's imperative that students studying for the Digital SAT® understand these foundational ideas. The properties, definitions, and uses of lines and angles are examined in this chapter, which lays the foundation for more complex geometry and trigonometry courses.

In geometry, lines are the most basic and fundamental objects. Any two points that lie on a line uniquely define it and allow it to expand eternally in both directions. Geometric concepts require a comprehension of several sorts of lines:

- **Parallel Lines**: Lines, regardless of length, in the same plane that never cross. Same slope characterizes parallel lines.
- **Perpendicular Lines**: Lines that meet at a 90-degree angle, or a right angle. Perpendicular line slopes are negative reciprocals of each other.
- **Intersecting Lines**: Line segments that intersect at any non-90 degree angle.

Example: If line l_1 has a slope of $m_1 = 2$, a line l_2 parallel to l_1 will also have a slope of 2. A line l_3 perpendicular to l_1 will have a slope of $-(1/2)$.

Angles: Types and Properties

Angles are formed by the intersection of two lines, rays, or segments. They are measured in degrees or radians, with a complete circle encompassing 360 degrees or 2π radians. The primary types of angles are:

- **Acute Angles**: Angles less than 90 degrees.
- **Right Angles**: Angles exactly 90 degrees.
- **Obtuse Angles**: Angles greater than 90 degrees but less than 180 degrees.
- **Straight Angles**: Angles exactly 180 degrees, forming a straight line.

Example: An angle measuring 45 degrees is an acute angle, while an angle measuring 135 degrees is an obtuse angle.

Angle Relationships and Theorems

Comprehending the correlations of angles is essential for resolving numerous geometric issues. Several key relationships and theorems include:

- **Adjacent Angles**: Angles that share a common vertex and side but do not overlap.
- **Vertical Angles**: Angles that cross when two lines come together. Vertical angles are always equal.
- **Complementary Angles**: Two angles, the sum of which is 90 degrees.
- **Supplementary Angles**: Two angles, the sum of which is 180 degrees.

Example: When two complimentary angles have one measure thirty degrees, the other must be sixty degrees. When two supplementary angles have one measurement of 110 degrees, the other angle needs to be 70 degrees.

Angle Bisectors

A line or ray that splits an angle into two equal portions is called an angle bisector. This concept is frequently used in geometric constructions and proofs.

Example: To bisect a 60-degree angle, one would create two 30-degree angles.

Transversals and Angle Pairs

Several angles are created when a transversal crosses two parallel lines, resulting in certain relationships:

- **Corresponding Angles**: Angles formed by a transversal that connects two parallel lines in matching corners. Angles that correspond are equal.
- **Alternate Interior Angles**: Angles inside the two lines but on different sides of the transversal. Alternate equal

interior angles.

- **Alternate Exterior Angles**: Angles outside of the two lines but on opposing sides of the transversal. The outside angles are equal.
- **Consecutive Interior Angles**: Angles on the same side of the transversal and inside the two lines. Consecutive interior angles are supplementary.

Example: If a transversal intersects two parallel lines creating a pair of corresponding angles, and one angle measures 50 degrees, the corresponding angle will also measure 50 degrees.

Calculating Angles
Geometry often involves calculating unknown angles based on given information. This typically requires applying the relationships and properties discussed above.
Example: Given that two angles are supplementary and one measures x degrees, the other angle measures 180 - x degrees.

Angle Sum Properties
Any polygon's interior angle sum can be computed using the number of sides as a basis:

- **Triangle**: The sum of the interior angles of a triangle is always 180 degrees.
- **Quadrilateral**: The sum of the interior angles of a quadrilateral is always 360 degrees.

Example: In a triangle with angles a, b, and c, the equation a + b + c = 180 holds. In a quadrilateral with angles a, b, c, and d, the equation a + b + c + d = 360 holds.

Angle Calculations in Triangles
In triangles, several specific properties and theorems are used to calculate angles:

- **Isosceles Triangle Theorem**: In an isosceles triangle, the base angles are equal.
- **Equilateral Triangle**: In an equilateral triangle, all three angles are equal, each measuring 60 degrees.
- **Exterior Angle Theorem**: The product of the measures of the two non-adjacent internal angles determines the measure of an exterior angle in a triangle.

Example: In an isosceles triangle with base angles measuring x degrees, the vertex angle measures 180 - 2x degrees.

Example Problems and Solutions

- **Problem**: Given two parallel lines cut by a transversal, if one of the alternate interior angles measures 3x + 10 degrees and the corresponding alternate interior angle measures 5x - 30 degrees, find the value of x.
  Solution: Since alternate interior angles are equal, we set up the equation: 3x + 10 = 5x - 30 Solving for x:
  3x + 10 = 5x − 30
  40 = 2x
  x = 20
- **Problem**: In a triangle, one angle measures 50 degrees, and another angle measures 60 degrees. Find the measure of the third angle.
  Solution: A triangle has 180 degrees total angles. Let the measure of the third angle be x:
  50 + 60 + x = 180
  x = 70
- **Problem**: If two angles are supplementary and one measures 2x + 30 degrees and the other measures 4x - 10 degrees, find the value of x.
  Solution: Since the angles are supplementary, their measures add up to 180 degrees:
  2x + 30 + 4x - 10 = 180
  6x + 20 = 180
  6x = 160
  x = 160/6
  x = 80/3

x approx 26.67

Gaining a solid understanding of lines and angles is necessary to learn geometry. These principles form the building blocks for more complex geometric concepts and applications, making them a critical component of the Digital SAT® preparation.

CALCULATING AREA, PERIMETER AND SCALE FACTORS

For Digital SAT® to be successful, a deep comprehension of area, perimeter, and scale factors is required. This chapter explores the definitions, formulas, and applications of these basic ideas in a variety of geometric shapes.

The volume that a shape occupies inside its boundaries is its area. Depending on the shape, there are several formulae and concepts to calculate the area, although some are universal.

Rectangles and Squares
For rectangles and squares, the area is calculated by multiplying the length and the width.
- **Rectangle**: $A = l \times w$
- **Square**: $A = s^2$

where l is the length, w is the width, and s is the side of the square.

Example: The width of a rectangle is 3 units, and its length is 8 units. Its area is 8 x 3 = 24 square units.

Triangles
The following formula can be used to find a triangle's area:
$A = \frac{1}{2} \times b \times h$
where b is the base, and h is the height.

Example: The area of a triangle having a base of 6 units and a height of 4 units is ½ x 6 x 4 = 12 square units.

Circles
The following formula can be used to find a circle's area:
$A = \pi r^2$
where r is the radius of the circle.

Example: A circle with a radius of 5 units has an area of $\pi \times 5^2 = 25\pi$ square units.

Parallelograms
The area of a parallelogram is calculated similarly to that of a rectangle:
$A = b \times h$
Where b is the base, and h is the height.

Example: A parallelogram with a base of 10 units and a height of 5 units has an area of 10 x 5 = 50 square units.

Trapezoids
For trapezoids, the area is given by:
$A = \frac{1}{2} \times (b_1 + b_2) \times h$
where the height is represented by h and the lengths of the two parallel sides are b1 and b2.

Example: The area of a trapezoid with bases of 8 and 5 and a height of 4 units is ½ x (8 + 5) x 4 = 26 square units.

Perimeter
The entire length of a shape's boundary is its perimeter. Different shapes require different methods to calculate the perimeter.

Rectangles and Squares

The perimeter of a rectangle and square can be calculated as follows:

- **Rectangle**: $P = 2l + 2w$
- **Square**: $P = 4s$

where l is the length, w is the width, and s is the side length.

Example: A rectangle with a length of 10 units and a width of 4 units has a perimeter of 2 x 10 + 2 x 4 = 28 units.

Triangles

The total of a triangle's side lengths determines its perimeter:
$P = a + b + c$
where a, b, and c are the lengths of the sides.

Example: A triangle with side lengths of 5 units, 6 units, and 7 units has a perimeter of 5 + 6 + 7 = 18 units.

Circles (Circumference)

The perimeter of a circle, known as the circumference, is given by:
$C = 2\pi r$
where r is the radius.

Example: A circle having a radius of 7 units has a circumference equal to 2π x 7 = 14π units.

Parallelograms

A parallelogram's perimeter is:
$P = 2a + 2b$
where the lengths of adjacent sides are denoted by a and b.

Example: A parallelogram with side lengths of 8 units and 5 units has a perimeter of 2 x 8 + 2 x 5 = 26 units.

Trapezoids

The total length of all a trapezoid's sides equals its perimeter:
$P = a + b_1 + b_2 + c$
where a, b_1, b_2, and c are the lengths of the sides.

Example: A trapezoid with side lengths of 3 units, 5 units, 6 units, and 7 units has a perimeter of 3 + 5 + 6 + 7 = 21 units.

Scale Factors

Scale factors are used to describe the proportional relationship between two similar geometric shapes. If one shape is an enlargement or reduction of another, the scale factor defines how much one shape has been scaled relative to the other.

Finding the Scale Factor

To find the scale factor between two similar shapes, divide the lengths of corresponding sides.
Example: If a rectangle has sides of 4 units and 6 units, and a similar rectangle has sides of 8 units and 12 units, the scale factor is:
Scale factor = 8/4 = 2

Applications of Scale Factors

Scale factors are crucial in many real-world applications, such as map reading, model building, and resizing images.
Example: An automobile is modelled at a 1:10 scale. If the actual car is 15 feet long, the model car will be:
Model length = 10/15 = 1.5 feet

Area and Volume Ratios

When dealing with areas and volumes of similar shapes, the scale factor impacts these measurements differently. The ratios for area and volume are equal to the square and cube of the scale factor, respectively.

Example: If the scale factor between two similar rectangles is 3, the ratio of their areas is:
Area ratio = 3^2 = 9
If the scale factor between two similar cubes is 2, the ratio of their volumes is:
Volume ratio = 2^3 = 8

Example Problems and Solutions

- **Problem**: Calculate the area and perimeter of a rectangle with a length of 12 units and a width of 9 units.
  Solution:
  Area: $A = l \times w = 12 \times 9 = 108$ square units.
  Perimeter: $P = 2l + 2w = 2 \times 12 + 2 \times 9 = 42$ units.
- **Problem**: A triangle has sides of 7 units, 24 units, and 25 units. Verify if it is a right triangle and calculate its area.
  Solution:
  Check right triangle: $7^2 + 24^2 = 49 + 576 = 625 = 25^2$. It is a right triangle.
  Area: $A = \frac{1}{2} \times b \times h = \frac{1}{2} \times 7 \times 24 = 84$ square units.
- **Problem**: Find the scale factor between two similar triangles if one has sides of 3 units, 4 units, and 5 units, and the other has sides of 6 units, 8 units, and 10 units.
  Solution: The scale factor is: Scale factor = 6/3 = 2
- **Problem**: A circular garden has a radius of 10 feet. Calculate its area and the circumference.
  Solution:
  Area: $A = \pi r^2 = \pi \times 10^2 = 100\pi$ square feet.
  Circumference: $C = 2\pi r = 2\pi \times 10 = 20\pi$ feet.

Students who grasp these basic ideas of area, perimeter, and scale factors will be better prepared to handle a range of geometric problems on the Digital SAT®. These ideas serve as the foundation for increasingly intricate computations and applications in both scholarly and practical settings.

PROPERTIES OF SIMILAR TRIANGLES

Understanding the characteristics of triangles, one of the most basic shapes in geometry, is essential for resolving a wide range of issues. In particular, similar triangles are important in a lot of geometric applications and proofs. This chapter will examine the attributes of comparable triangles, emphasizing their distinguishing features, property-related theorems, and real-world uses.

If two triangles are comparable in shape—but not always in size—they are said to be similar. This indicates that the lengths of similar sides are proportionate and that corresponding angles are equal. There are several ways to assess triangle resemblance:

- **Angle-Angle (AA) Similarity**: The triangles are comparable if their two angles are the same as those of another triangle.
- **Side-Angle-Side (SAS) Similarity**: Triangles are considered comparable if two triangles have identical angles and their side lengths are proportionate.
- **Side-Side-Side (SSS) Similarity**: Two triangles are comparable if their matching sides are proportionate.

Properties of Similar Triangles

For many geometric problems, the properties of similar triangles are crucial. Here are some key properties:

- **Corresponding Angles are Equal**: In similar triangles, all corresponding angles are congruent. If
  $\triangle ABC \sim \triangle DEF$, then $\angle A = \angle D$, $\angle B = \angle E$, and $\angle C = \angle F$.

- **Corresponding Sides are Proportional**: Similar triangles have comparable lengths for their respective sides. If $\triangle ABC \sim \triangle DEF$, then $\frac{AB}{DE} = \frac{BC}{EF} = \frac{CA}{FD}$.

- **Ratio of Perimeters**: Any two equivalent side lengths can be expressed as the ratio of the perimeters of any two similar triangles.

$$\frac{\text{Perimeter of } \triangle ABC}{\text{Perimeter of } \triangle DEF} = \frac{AB}{DE}$$

- **Ratio of Areas**: If two triangles are similar to one other, then their area ratio is equal to the square of their respective side length ratios.

$$\frac{\text{Area of } \triangle ABC}{\text{Area of } \triangle DEF} = \left(\frac{AB}{DE}\right)^2$$

Theorems Involving Similar Triangles

Several important theorems involve similar triangles and their properties. These theorems are often used to solve complex geometric problems.

1. Basic Proportionality Theorem (Thales' Theorem): A triangle's sides are divided proportionately if a line drawn parallel to one side intersects the other two sides.

If $\overline{DE} \parallel \overline{BC}$ in $\triangle ABC$, then:

$$\frac{AD}{DB} = \frac{AE}{EC}$$

2. Converse of Basic Proportionality Theorem: Lines that divide two triangle sides proportionately run parallel to the third side.

3. Angle Bisector Theorem: The opposing side of a triangle is divided into segments that are proportionate to the other two sides by the angle bisector of that angle.

If $\overline{AD}$ is the angle bisector of $\angle BAC$ in $\triangle ABC$, then:

$$\frac{BD}{DC} = \frac{AB}{AC}$$

Practical Applications of Similar Triangles

Similar triangles are used in various practical applications, from architectural design to astronomical measurements. Below are a few examples illustrating their practical use:

1. Indirect Measurement: Similar triangles can be used to find distances or heights that are difficult to measure directly. For instance, if you want to find the height of a tree, you can use a smaller, measurable object to form similar triangles.

Example: Let's say a tree throws a shadow of 9.6 meters and a person 1.8 meters tall casts a shadow of 2.4 meters. We can set up the proportion:

$$\frac{\text{Height of person}}{\text{Shadow of person}} = \frac{\text{Height of tree}}{\text{Shadow of tree}}$$

$$\frac{1.8}{2.4} = \frac{h}{9.6}$$

Solving for (h):

$$h = \frac{1.8 \times 9.6}{2.4} = 7.2 \text{ meters}$$

Thus, the height of the tree is 7.2 meters.

2. Map Reading and Scale Models: Similar triangles are used in map reading and creating scale models. The scale factor is a key concept here.

Example: If a map scale states that 1 cm on the map represents 100 meters in real life, and the distance between two points on the map is 5 cm, the actual distance is:

Actual distance = 5 cm x 100 meters/cm = 500 meters

3. Shadows and Light: In the study of light and shadows, similar triangles can help determine the length of shadows cast by objects.

Example: A 20-meter-tall skyscraper creates a 30-meter-long shadow. A flagpole creates a 15-meter-long shadow at the same moment. To find the height of the flagpole (h), we use the proportion:

$$\frac{\text{Height of building}}{\text{Shadow of building}} = \frac{\text{Height of flagpole}}{\text{Shadow of flagpole}}$$

$$\frac{20}{30} = \frac{h}{15}$$

Solving for (h):

$$h = \frac{20 \times 15}{30} = 10 \text{ meters}$$

Thus, the flagpole is 10 meters tall.

Comprehending the characteristics of comparable triangles is essential for addressing an array of queries on the Digital SAT®. Your ability to use proportional reasoning, identify similarities, and find unknown lengths or angles will frequently be put to the test in these situations. Understanding these ideas improves one's ability to solve mathematical problems in general as well as in geometry classes.

To sum up, comparable triangles are a basic idea in geometry with a wide range of uses. Students can greatly enhance their SAT® scores and gain a greater understanding of geometric fundamentals by comprehending these qualities and working through related tasks.

UNDERSTANDING THE PYTHAGOAREN THEOREM

One of the most well-known and frequently applied geometrical principles is the Pythagorean Theorem. This theorem, named for the Greek mathematician Pythagoras, is fundamental to many mathematical and practical applications. The formulation, proof, and applications of the theorem will all be covered in this chapter, giving you a thorough grasp that is essential to mastering the Digital SAT®.

In a right-angled triangle, the Pythagorean Theorem states that the square of the length of the hypotenuse, or side opposite the right angle, is equal to the sum of the squares of the lengths of the other two sides. In terms of math, this is expressed as:

$c^2 = a^2 + b^2$

where the other two sides of the triangle are a and b, and c is the length of the hypotenuse.

Imagine a right-angled triangle with sides a and b and a hypotenuse of c to intuitively understand the Pythagorean Theorem. The area of the square on the hypotenuse (c^2), if squares are built on each of these three sides, will exactly equal the sum of the areas of the squares on the other two sides (a^2) and (b^2).

Proof of the Pythagorean Theorem

There are numerous proofs of the Pythagorean Theorem, reflecting its fundamental nature in mathematics. Here, we present a classic geometric proof.

- **Constructing the Squares**: Begin with a right-angled triangle $\triangle ABC$ with right angle at C. Construct a square on each side of the triangle. Label the sides such that AB = c, AC = b, and BC = a.
- **Rearranging the Triangles**: Construct a larger square with side a + b, which can be divided into four copies of $\triangle ABC$ and two smaller squares with sides a and b. The area of the large square is $(a + b)^2$.

- **Calculating the Areas**: The area of the large square can also be expressed as the sum of the areas of the four triangles and the two smaller squares:

$$(a + b)^2 = 4\left(\tfrac{1}{2}ab\right) + a^2 + b^2$$

Simplifying, we get:

$$(a + b)^2 = 2ab + a^2 + b^2$$

- **Equating the Areas**: Since both expressions represent the area of the same large square, we can set them equal: $(a + b)^2 = 2ab + a^2 + b^2$. Expanding the left side: $a^2 + 2ab + b^2 = 2ab + a^2 + b^2$. Subtracting 2ab from both sides, we obtain: $a^2 + b^2 = c^2$

This proof illustrates the relationship between the areas, reinforcing the truth of the Pythagorean Theorem.

Applications of the Pythagorean Theorem

The Pythagorean Theorem is not merely an abstract mathematical principle; it has numerous practical applications across various fields.

1. **Distance Calculation**: The theorem is frequently used to calculate distances, particularly in coordinate geometry. For instance, to determine the distance between two points (x_1, y_1) and (x_2, y_2) in a plane, we can use the distance formula derived from the Pythagorean Theorem:

$$d = \sqrt{(x_2 - x_1)^2 + (y_2 - y_1)^2}$$

   This application is crucial in fields such as physics, engineering, and computer graphics.
   Example: Calculate the distance between the points (3, 4) and (7, 1).
   Solution:
$$d = \sqrt{(7 - 3)^2 + (1 - 4)^2} = \sqrt{4^2 + (-3)^2} = \sqrt{16 + 9} = \sqrt{25} = 5$$
   Thus, the distance between the points is 5 units.

2. **Construction and Architecture**: The Pythagorean Theorem is used in architecture and construction to determine diagonal distances and to guarantee that right angles are accurate. For instance, the theorem aids in confirming the layout's rectangularity when creating a building's foundation.
   Example: A rectangular plot of land measures 30 meters by 40 meters. Calculate the length of the diagonal.
   Solution: Using the Pythagorean Theorem:

$$d = \sqrt{30^2 + 40^2} = \sqrt{900 + 1600} = \sqrt{2500} = 50 \text{ meters}$$

3. **Trigonometry and Navigation**: The Pythagorean Theorem is foundational in trigonometry, particularly in the definition of trigonometric functions for right-angled triangles. It also aids in navigation, allowing for the calculation of direct routes and bearings.
   Example: A ship sails 6 miles east and then 8 miles north. Calculate the direct distance from the starting point.

$$d = \sqrt{6^2 + 8^2} = \sqrt{36 + 64} = \sqrt{100} = 10 \text{ miles}$$
   Solution:

4. **Surveying and Mapping**: Surveyors use the Pythagorean Theorem to measure inaccessible distances and to create accurate maps. The theorem helps in triangulating positions and calculating heights indirectly.
   Example: To find the height of a hill, a surveyor measures a horizontal distance of 100 meters from the base to a point directly under the summit and finds the angle of elevation to be 30 degrees. Using trigonometry and the Pythagorean Theorem:

$$\text{Height} = 100 \times \tan(30°) = 100 \times \tfrac{1}{\sqrt{3}} \approx 57.7 \text{ meters}$$

Proofs and Variations

Beyond the standard geometric proof, the Pythagorean Theorem can be demonstrated using algebraic methods and dissection proofs. These variations highlight the theorem's robustness and versatility.

- **Algebraic Proof**: Consider two squares, one with side length c and another with side length a + b. By arranging four right-angled triangles within the larger square, we can derive the theorem algebraically as shown earlier.

- **Dissection Proof**: A classic dissection proof involves rearranging parts of the squares on the triangle's legs to form the square on the hypotenuse. This visual proof emphasizes the theorem's geometric elegance.

Extensions and Generalizations

The Pythagorean Theorem extends beyond two dimensions and right-angled triangles. In three dimensions, the distance between two points in space can be calculated using:

$$d = \sqrt{(x_2 - x_1)^2 + (y_2 - y_1)^2 + (z_2 - z_1)^2}$$

Moreover, the theorem generalizes to other geometric shapes and higher dimensions through the use of vector algebra and the dot product.

Example: Calculate the distance between the points (1, 2, 3) and (4, 6, 8) in three-dimensional space.

Solution:

$$d = \sqrt{(4 - 1)^2 + (6 - 2)^2 + (8 - 3)^2} = \sqrt{3^2 + 4^2 + 5^2} = \sqrt{9 + 16 + 25} = \sqrt{50} \approx 7.07$$

In geometry, the Pythagorean Theorem is still fundamental since it provides knowledge and resources needed for both theoretical and applied mathematics. Students who grasp this theorem will be better equipped to solve problems and comprehend geometric relationships, which will help them succeed on the Digital SAT® and other tests.

CHARACTERISTICS OF SPECIAL RIGHT TRIANGLES

Geometric principles rely heavily on special right triangles, especially when applied to the Digital SAT®. These triangles provide streamlined computations and problem-solving strategies because of their distinct characteristics and precise angle measurements. The main features of special right triangles are examined in this chapter, with particular attention to the 45-45-90 and 30-60-90 triangles, which are commonly found in a variety of mathematical contexts.

45-45-90 Triangles

The 45-45-90 triangle, sometimes referred to as the isosceles right triangle, has two 45-degree angles and one 90-degree angle. The computations involving the sides of this triangle are made easier by their constant ratio.

The legs of a 45-45-90 triangle are congruent, and the hypotenuse measures $\sqrt{2}$ times the length of each leg. If each leg is of length x, then the hypotenuse h can be expressed as: $h = x\sqrt{2}$

Example Problem

Given a 45-45-90 triangle with legs of length 5, find the length of the hypotenuse.

Solution: $h = 5\sqrt{2}$ Thus, the hypotenuse is $5\sqrt{2}$.

Derivation from the Pythagorean Theorem

A 45-45-90 triangle's side length relationship can be determined by applying the Pythagorean Theorem. Assume that c is the triangle's hypotenuse and that a and b are its legs. Since $a = b$:

$c^2 = a^2 + b^2$
$c^2 = a^2 + a^2$
$c^2 = 2a^2$
$c = a\sqrt{2}$

This confirms that the hypotenuse is $\sqrt{2}$ times the length of each leg.

The 45-45-90 triangle's simplicity makes it useful in various scenarios, including geometry problems involving squares and regular octagons. Without the use of trigonometric functions, its constant side ratios allow for speedy computations.

30-60-90 Triangles

The 30-60-90 triangle is another special right triangle with distinctive properties. It has angles of 30 degrees, 60 degrees, and 90 degrees. The side lengths of this triangle follow a specific ratio that aids in solving problems efficiently.

In a 30-60-90 triangle, the length of the hypotenuse is twice that of the shorter leg, and the length of the longer leg is $\sqrt{3}$ times the shorter leg. If the shorter leg is x, then the longer leg l and the hypotenuse h are:

h = 2x

l = x$\sqrt{3}$

Example Problem

Given a 30-60-90 triangle with the shorter leg of length 4, find the lengths of the longer leg and the hypotenuse.

Solution:

h = 2 x 4 = 8

l = 4$\sqrt{3}$

Thus, the hypotenuse is 8 and the longer leg is 4$\sqrt{3}$.

Derivation from Equilateral Triangles

An equilateral triangle can be converted to a 30-60-90 triangle by measuring the altitude between one vertex and the opposite side's midpoint. The equilateral triangle is divided into two congruent triangles measuring 30-60-90 by this altitude. Assume that the equilateral triangle has two sides, 2a. This side is divided into two length a segments by the altitude, forming two right triangles. The altitude, being the longer leg, is: l = a$\sqrt{3}$

The hypotenuse remains 2a, and the shorter leg is a.

The 30-60-90 triangle's predictable side ratios make it particularly useful in problems involving equilateral triangles and hexagons. It also frequently appears in trigonometric problems where these specific angles are involved.

Comparing 45-45-90 and 30-60-90 Triangles

Although both varieties of special right triangles provide easier computations, their uses vary according to the ratios of their side lengths to angles. Students can identify and use these triangles in a variety of geometric and trigonometric problems by being aware of their properties.

Special right triangles are important in situations involving congruence and likeness. It is possible to identify and solve these issues quickly when one is aware of the precise ratios of their sides. For instance, using the established ratios, one may quickly ascertain the remaining sides given the lengths of some of the sides.

Example Problem

Determine whether the triangles with sides (7, 7, 7$\sqrt{2}$) and (14, 14, 14$\sqrt{2}$) are similar.

Solution: The sides of both triangles are in the ratio 1:1:$\sqrt{2}$, indicating that both are 45-45-90 triangles. According to the Side-Side-Side (SSS) similarity criterion, they are thus comparable.

CIRCLE PROPERTIES

One of the main aspects of geometry that is necessary to solve a variety of problems on the Digital SAT® is an understanding of the properties of circles. This chapter explores the essential characteristics of circles, looking at their main elements, the connections between them, and the equations that control their behavior. Students who fully comprehend these traits will be able to respond to inquiries about circles with assurance and accuracy.

All points on a plane that are uniformly distanced from the center, a fixed point, make up a circle. The length of the circle, measured from the center to any point on the circle, is known as the radius. The diameter, which connects two locations on the circle, is twice the radius and goes through the center. The circle's perimeter, often known as its boundary, is its circumference.

- **Radius (r):** The radius is a crucial component, as many properties and formulas of a circle are derived from it. The radius extends from the center to any point on the circle.
- **Diameter (d):** The diameter is twice the length of the radius and passes through the center, connecting two points on the circumference. It can be expressed as: d = 2r
- **Circumference (C):** The circumference is the total length around the circle. It can be calculated using the radius or diameter with the following formulas:
  C = 2πr
  C = πd

Example Problem: Calculate the circumference of a circle with a radius of 7 cm.
Solution: C = 2π7 = 14π. Thus, the circumference is 14π cm.

Arc and Arc Length

A circle's circumference includes an arc. An arc's length is determined by the central angle, θ, that it subtends. The arc length L can be calculated using the formula:

$$L = \frac{\theta}{360} \times 2\pi r$$

or

$$L = \frac{\theta}{360} \times \pi d$$

Example Problem: Find the length of an arc with a central angle of 60 degrees in a circle with a radius of 10 cm.
Solution:

$$L = \frac{60}{360} \times 2\pi \times 10 = \frac{1}{6} \times 20\pi = \frac{20\pi}{6} = \frac{10\pi}{3}$$

Thus, the arc length is $\frac{10\pi}{3}$ cm.

- **Chord:** Line segments having both ends on a circle are called chords. A unique kind of chord known as the diameter goes through the circle's center.
- **Tangent:** A straight line touching a circle exactly once is called a tangent to the circle. We refer to this location as the tangency point. At the point of tangency, the tangent and radius are perpendicular.
- **Secant:** A line that crosses the circle twice is called a secant.

Area of a Circle

The area that a circle's circumference encloses is known as area A. It can be calculated using the formula: A = πr²
Example Problem: Calculate the area of a circle with a radius of 5 cm.
Solution: A = π x 5² = 25π. Thus, the area is 25π cm².

Sector of a Circle

A sector is the portion of a circle that has two radii and the matching arc surrounding it. The radius r and the central angle θ can be used to compute a sector asector's area:

$$A_{sector} = \frac{\theta}{360} \times \pi r^2$$

Example Problem: Determine the size of a sector in a circle with a radius of 8 cm that has a central angle of 90 degrees.

Solution: $A_{sector} = \frac{90}{360} \times \pi \times 8^2 = \frac{1}{4} \times \pi \times 64 = 16\pi$ .Thus, the area of the sector is 16π cm².

Equations of a Circle

In coordinate geometry, the equation of a circle with center h, k and radius r is: $(x - h)^2 + (y - k)^2 = r^2$

Example Problem: Write the equation of a circle with center (3, -2) and radius 5.

Solution: $(x - 3)^2 + (y + 2)^2 = 25$

Intersecting Chords Theorem

The products of the segment lengths of two chords intersecting inside a circle equalize. If two chords AB and CD intersect at point E, then: AE x EB = CE x ED]

Example Problem: Given that chord AB and chord CD intersect at point E, where AE = 4 cm, EB = 6 cm, and CE = 3 cm, find the length of ED.

Solution: Using the intersecting chords theorem:

AE x EB = CE x ED

4 x 6 = 3 x ED

24 = 3 x ED

ED = 8

Thus, the length of ED is 8 cm.

Tangent and Radius

When a circle tangents to the radius, the tangent is perpendicular to the radius. Solving tangent and circle-related problems can be aided by this property.

Example Problem: A tangent to a circle at point A has a radius OA of 10 cm. If a line segment from point O to a point on the tangent is 26 cm long, find the distance from the center to the point where the line segment intersects the tangent.

Solution: Let the point where the line segment intersects the tangent be B. Since OA is perpendicular to the tangent at A, triangle OAB is a right triangle. Using the Pythagorean theorem:

$OB^2 = OA^2 + AB^2$

$26^2 = 10^2 + AB^2$

$676 = 100 + AB^2$

$AB^2 = 576$

$AB = 24$

Thus, the distance from the center to the point where the line segment intersects the tangent is 24 cm.

Inscribed Angles

A circle's two chords that share an endpoint produce an inscribed angle. Half of the intercepted arc's measure equals the measure of an inscribed angle.

Example Problem: Find the measure of an inscribed angle that intercepts an arc of 100 degrees.

Solution: The measure of the inscribed angle is half the measure of the intercepted arc: Inscribed Angle = 100/2 = 50 degrees

Central Angles

An angle is said to be central if its sides are radii and its vertex is found at the center of the circle. The intercepted arc measure of a central angle equals the angle's measure.

Example Problem: Find the measure of the central angle that intercepts an arc of 150 degrees.

Solution: The measure of the central angle is equal to the measure of the intercepted arc: Central Angle = 150 degrees

EXPLORING THREE-DIMENSIONAL SHAPES

Three-dimensional shapes in geometry bring a new level of complexity and richness to solving mathematical puzzles. Comprehending these forms is essential for addressing multiple topics on the Digital SAT®, since they incorporate ideas of volume, surface area, and spatial thinking. This chapter explores the fundamental qualities of three-dimensional shapes, including their traits, equations, and real-world uses.

Different from two-dimensional figures, three-dimensional shapes, also called solids, include depth in addition to length and width. Vertices, edges, and faces are these shapes' main building blocks.

- **Vertices**: Points where edges meet.
- **Edges**: Line segments where faces intersect.
- **Faces**: Flat surfaces that make up the boundary of the solid.

Common three-dimensional shapes include prisms, cylinders, pyramids, cones, and spheres. The volume and surface area of each of these forms are determined by certain formulas and characteristics.

Prisms

Three-dimensional prisms consist of two congruent, parallel bases joined by rectangular faces. The type of prism is determined by the shape of its base.

- **Rectangular Prism**: Has rectangular bases.
- **Triangular Prism**: Has triangular bases.

The Prism's Volume

The area of the prism's base B multiplied by its height h yields the volume V of the prism: V is equal to B times h.

Surface Area of a Prism

The total area of all the faces is known as SA. This may be determined using the formula $SA = 2lw + 2lh + 2wh$ for a rectangular prism, where l is the length, w is the width, and h is the height.

Example Problem: With a rectangular prism that measures 4 cm in length, 3 cm in width, and 5 cm in height, find its volume and surface area.

Solution:

$V = l \times w \times h = 4 \times 3 \times 5 = 60$ cm³

$SA = 2(4 \times 3) + 2(4 \times 5) + 2(3 \times 5) = 2(12) + 2(20) + 2(15) = 24 + 40 + 30 = 94$ cm²

Cylinders

Cylinders have two parallel, congruent circular bases connected by a curved surface.

Volume of a Cylinder

The formula for calculating a cylinder's volume, $V = \pi r^2 h$, takes into account the height (h) and the base's radius (r).

Surface Area of a Cylinder

The surface area SA is the sum of the areas of the two bases and the curved surface: $SA = 2\pi r(h + r)$

Example Problem: Find the volume and surface area of a cylinder with a radius of 3 cm and a height of 7 cm.

Solution:

$V = \pi \times 3^2 \times 7 = 63\pi$ cm³

$SA = 2\pi \times 3 \times (7 + 3) = 2\pi \times 3 \times 10 = 60\pi$ cm²

Pyramids

Pyramids have a polygonal base and triangular faces that converge at a single point called the apex.

Volume of a Pyramid

$V = (1/3)Bh$ is the formula for calculating a pyramid's volume V which denotes the height from the base to the apex (h) and the area of the base (B).

Surface Area of a Pyramid
The surface area SA is the sum of the base area and the areas of the triangular faces.
Example Problem: Find the volume of a pyramid with a square base of side length 4 cm and a height of 6 cm.
Solution:
B = 4 x 4 = 16 cm²
V = 1/3 x 16 x 6 = 32 cm³

Cones
Cones feature a curving surface that tapers to a point known as the apex, and a round base.

Volume of a Cone
The volume V of a cone is: V = (1/3)πr²h

Surface Area of a Cone
The surface area SA includes the base area and the lateral surface area:

SA = πr (r + l) where l is the slant height, calculated as: $l = \sqrt{r^2 + h^2}$
Example Problem: Find the volume and surface area of a cone with a radius of 3 cm and a height of 4 cm.
Solution:
$$V = \tfrac{1}{3}\pi \times 3^2 \times 4 = 12\pi \text{ cm}^3$$
$$l = \sqrt{3^2 + 4^2} = 5 \text{ cm}$$
$$SA = \pi \times 3 \times (3 + 5) = 24\pi \text{ cm}^2$$

Spheres
Spheres are perfectly symmetrical three-dimensional shapes where all points on the surface are equidistant from the center.

Volume of a Sphere
The volume V of a sphere is calculated using: V = (4/3)πr³

Surface Area of a Sphere
The surface area SA is: SA = 4πr²
Example Problem: Find the volume and surface area of a sphere with a radius of 6 cm.
Solution:
$$V = \tfrac{4}{3}\pi \times 6^3 = 288\pi \text{ cm}^3$$
$$SA = 4\pi \times 6^2 = 144\pi \text{ cm}^2$$

Composite Solids
Two or more straightforward three-dimensional shapes combine to form composite solids. Composite solids can be found by disassembling them into smaller parts, computing the necessary measurements for each component, then combining the results to determine their volume or surface area.
Example Problem: Determine the volume of a composite solid that is made up of a 3 cm diameter, 5 cm height cylinder and a hemisphere that is affixed to the top of the cylinder.
Solution: First, calculate the volume of the cylinder: $V_{cylinder} = \pi \times 3^2 \times 5 = 45\pi$ cm³

Next, calculate the volume of the hemisphere (half of a sphere): $V_{hemisphere} = \tfrac{1}{2} \times \tfrac{4}{3}\pi \times 3^3 = 18\pi \text{ cm}^3$
Add the volumes together: $V_{composite} = 45\pi + 18\pi = 63\pi$ cm³

TRIGONOMETRIC RATIOS: SINE, COSINE AND TANGENT

Geometry's most important subject, trigonometry, examines the connections between triangles' angles and sides. Right triangle issues need the use of the fundamental trigonometric ratios, sine, cosine, and tangent. A thorough examination of these ratios, their meanings, and their uses in diverse situations are given in this chapter.

Trigonometric ratios are based on the angles and sides of a right triangle. A right triangle has one angle of 90 degrees, and the trigonometric ratios are defined for one of the other two angles, typically denoted as θ (theta).

- **Hypotenuse:** The side opposite the right angle, and the longest side of the triangle.
- **Opposite Side:** The side opposite the angle θ.
- **Adjacent Side:** The side adjacent to the angle θ and not the hypotenuse.

The three primary trigonometric ratios are defined as follows:

1. **Sine (sin θ):**

$$\sin \theta = \frac{\text{Opposite}}{\text{Hypotenuse}}$$

2. **Cosine (cos θ):**

$$\cos \theta = \frac{\text{Adjacent}}{\text{Hypotenuse}}$$

3. **Tangent (tan θ):**

$$\tan \theta = \frac{\text{Opposite}}{\text{Adjacent}}$$

Using Trigonometric Ratios

Understanding the Pythagorean Theorem, which asserts that $a2 + b2 = c2$ where c is the hypotenuse and a and b are the other two sides, and the fundamental characteristics of right triangles are necessary in order to use trigonometric ratios efficiently.

Example Problem: Given a right triangle where the hypotenuse is 10 units and one of the legs is 6 units, find the sine, cosine, and tangent of the angle opposite the 6-unit leg.

Solution: First, find the length of the other leg using the Pythagorean Theorem:

$a2 + 62 = 102$

$a2 + 36 = 100$

$a2 = 64$

$a = 8$

Now, calculate the trigonometric ratios

$$\sin \theta = \frac{\text{Opposite}}{\text{Hypotenuse}} = \frac{6}{10} = 0.6$$

$$\cos \theta = \frac{\text{Adjacent}}{\text{Hypotenuse}} = \frac{8}{10} = 0.8$$

$$\tan \theta = \frac{\text{Opposite}}{\text{Adjacent}} = \frac{6}{8} = 0.75$$

Inverse Trigonometric Functions

Inverse trigonometric functions allow us to find the angle when given a trigonometric ratio. These functions are denoted as arcsine $\sin^{-1}$, arccosine $\cos^{-1}$, and arctangent $\tan^{-1}$.

Example Problem:

Find the angle θ if $\sin\theta = 0.5$.

Solution:

$$\theta = \sin^{-1}(0.5)$$

Using a calculator, we find:

$$\theta = 30°$$

Applications of Trigonometric Ratios

Trigonometric ratios are used in various applications, from solving triangles to modeling periodic phenomena.

Solving Triangles

Given some parts of a triangle, we can use trigonometric ratios to find unknown angles or sides.

Example Problem: A ladder is leaning against a wall, forming a 75-degree angle with the ground. If the ladder is 15 feet long, how high does it reach on the wall?

Solution: Using the cosine ratio:

$$\cos 75° = \frac{\text{Adjacent}}{15}$$

$$\text{Adjacent} = 15\cos 75°$$

$$\text{Adjacent} \approx 15 \times 0.2588 \approx 3.88 \text{ feet}$$

Unit Circle and Trigonometric Functions

Comprehending trigonometric functions requires an understanding of the unit circle. A circle with a radius of one unit and its center at the origin of a coordinate plane is called a unit circle. The sine and cosine of an angle are defined using the coordinates of points on the unit circle.

Unit Circle Definitions:

- The x-coordinate of a point on the unit circle is the cosine of the angle.
- The y-coordinate is the sine of the angle.

For example, the point corresponding to a 45-degree angle (or $\pi/4$ radians) on the unit circle has coordinates $\left(\frac{\sqrt{2}}{2}, \frac{\sqrt{2}}{2}\right)$. Thus:

$$\cos 45° = \frac{\sqrt{2}}{2}$$
$$\sin 45° = \frac{\sqrt{2}}{2}$$

Graphing Trigonometric Functions

Graphing sine, cosine, and tangent functions helps visualize their periodic nature and understand their behavior.

Sine and Cosine Functions

The graphs of sine and cosine functions are wave-like and periodic, repeating every 2π radians (360 degrees).

y =sin x

y =cos x

These functions oscillate between -1 and 1, with the sine function starting at (0, 0) and the cosine function starting at (0, 1).

Tangent Function

The tangent function, defined as the ratio of sine to cosine, has a periodicity of π radians (180 degrees).

y = tan x

The tangent function has vertical asymptotes where the cosine function is zero (e.g., at x = $\pi/2$, $3\pi/2$).

Example Problem: Sketch the graph of $y = \sin x$ and $y = \cos x$ over one period (0 to 2π).

Solution:

For $y = \sin x$:

- Starts at (0, 0)
- Peaks at ($\pi/2$, 1)
- Crosses zero at (π, 0)
- Troughs at ($3\pi/2$, -1)
- Returns to zero at (2π, 0)

For $y = \cos x$:

- Starts at (0, 1)
- Crosses zero at ($\pi/2$, 0)
- Troughs at (π, -1)
- Crosses zero at ($3\pi/2$, 0)
- Returns to the peak at (2π, 1)

Comprehending and acquiring proficiency in trigonometric ratios is important for addressing an extensive array of mathematical and scientific challenges. Students can establish a strong foundation for the trigonometric problems on the Digital SAT® by practicing and applying these ideas.

CHAPTER 14: SAT® READING AND WRITING - COMPREHENSION AND ANALYSIS

QUESTIONS ON MAIN IDEAS

It is essential to comprehend the primary concepts in a passage in order to perform well on the SAT® Reading and Writing part. The purpose of main concept questions is to assess your comprehension of the main idea or central subject that the author is attempting to express. This section will address several strategies and techniques for mastering these types of questions.

A passage's primary concept is its most significant point or contention. It's what the writer wants you to take away from the book and keep in mind. You must look for the underlying topic that unites every section of the paragraph in order to determine its core notion.

Example Passage: "The late 1700s and early 1800s saw a significant industrialization period known as the Industrial Revolution. During this period, nations underwent significant economic and technological transformation, evolving from agrarian economies to industrial superpowers. The introduction of machinery, such as the steam engine, and innovations in manufacturing processes led to mass production, which significantly boosted productivity and economic growth. This period also saw the rise of factories, which changed the nature of work and led to the urbanization of populations. However, the Industrial Revolution also brought about significant social challenges, including poor working conditions and environmental degradation."

In this example, the main idea is the transformation and impact of the Industrial Revolution on society and the economy. The passage discusses the technological advancements, economic changes, and social challenges that occurred during this period.

Techniques for Identifying Main Ideas
1. **Summarize the passage**: Try to sum up the passage in your own words after you've read it. Focus on the most important points and see if you can capture the essence of what the author is trying to convey.
2. **Look for Repeated Ideas**: Main ideas are often emphasized through repetition. If a particular concept or theme is mentioned multiple times, it is likely to be the main idea.
3. **Pay Attention to the First and Last Paragraphs**: Authors often introduce the main idea in the opening paragraph and reinforce it in the conclusion. These sections can provide valuable clues about the central theme.
4. **Identify Topic Sentences**: Topic sentences, usually found at the beginning of paragraphs, often state the main idea of that paragraph. By identifying the topic sentences, you can piece together the main idea of the entire passage.
5. **Ask Yourself Questions**: Consider questions like "What is the author trying to tell me?" or "What does the author want me to comprehend above all else?" These questions can guide you toward the main idea.

Common Pitfalls and How to Avoid Them
*   **Focusing on Details Instead of the Big Picture**: It's easy to get bogged down in specific details and miss the main idea. Always take a step back and evaluate how the specifics fit within the passage's overall framework.
*   **Confusing Supporting Details with the Main Idea**: Although they represent examples or proof to support the major notion, supporting details do not constitute the core idea in and of themselves. Ensure you differentiate between the two.
*   **Misinterpreting the Author's Purpose**: Understanding the author's purpose can help you identify the main idea. Is the writer attempting to educate, convince, amuse, or clarify? The purpose often aligns closely with the main idea.

Practice Questions
Question 1: What is the main idea of the following passage?

"One of the most important problems facing humanity right now is climate change. Natural catastrophes including hurricanes, floods, and wildfires are occurring more frequently and with greater severity as a result of rising global temperatures. Sea levels are rising as a result of the polar ice caps melting, endangering coastal populations all over the world. In addition, ecosystems are being disrupted by climate change, endangering food security and causing a loss of biodiversity. Coordinated international action is needed to address this issue by lowering greenhouse gas emissions and switching to renewable energy sources."

Answer: The main idea of the passage is that climate change is a significant and urgent problem that requires global action to mitigate its effects.

Question 2: Which of the following sums up the passage's primary point the best?

A. Sea levels are rising due to the melting of the polar ice caps.
B. Both the frequency and severity of natural disasters are rising.
C. Climate change poses numerous threats and requires global action.
D. Biodiversity loss is a major consequence of climate change.

Answer: C. Climate change poses numerous threats and requires global action.

Strategies for Answering Main Idea Questions
- **Read the Entire Passage**: Ensure you read the entire passage before attempting to answer main idea questions. Understanding the full context is essential.
- **Eliminate Incorrect Options**: To reduce your options, apply the process of elimination. Discard options that are too narrow or too broad, and focus on the ones that best capture the essence of the passage.
- **Look for Keywords and Phrases**: Pay attention to keywords and phrases that signal the main idea, such as "primarily," "most importantly," "central," and "mainly."
- **Refer Back to the Passage**: If you're unsure, refer back to the passage to find evidence that supports your choice. This can assist you in verifying that you have located the right primary notion.

Advanced Techniques
1. **Synthesize Information**: In some passages, the main idea is not explicitly stated but must be inferred by synthesizing information from different parts of the text. Practice combining clues to arrive at a coherent understanding of the main idea.
2. **Recognize the Author's Perspective**: Take into account the tone and viewpoint of the author. Understanding whether the author is supportive, critical, neutral, or enthusiastic about the topic can provide insights into the main idea.
3. **Distinguish Between Main Idea and Theme**: While the main idea is the specific point the author is making, the theme is a broader, more abstract concept. For example, a passage about the dangers of deforestation may have a main idea related to environmental conservation, while the theme could be the conflict between economic development and environmental protection.

You can enhance your comprehension abilities and score higher on the SAT® Reading and Writing portion by becoming proficient in the methods of identifying important concepts. Regular practice with a variety of passages can help you become skilled at identifying the main ideas and points made by authors.

SPECIFIC DETAIL QUESTIONS

The purpose of the SAT® Reading and Writing section's specific detail questions is to assess your capacity to recognize and understand distinct ideas within a passage. These inquiries frequently center on data, numbers, instances, and other specifics that bolster the author's major points or arguments. It takes an acute attention to detail as well as fast searching and interpretation of pertinent information to master these kinds of queries.

Generally speaking, specific detail questions focus on a single sentence, phrase, or paragraph in the passage. Frequently, they start with "According to the passage," "The author mentions," or "Which of the following is true about." You must identify or recollect specific facts and comprehend its context within the passage in order to answer these questions.

Example Passage: "In the late 19th century, the city of Paris underwent a significant transformation. Under the direction of Baron Haussmann, wide boulevards replaced narrow, winding streets, and new parks and public spaces were created. This modernization effort was part of a broader movement to improve urban living conditions and accommodate a growing population. The changes not only enhanced the aesthetic appeal of Paris but also improved sanitation and reduced the spread of disease."

Example Question: "According to the passage, what was one of the reasons for the modernization of Paris under Baron Haussmann?"

Answer: "To improve urban living conditions and accommodate a growing population."

Strategies for Answering Specific Detail Questions
1. **Carefully Read the Question**: Take special note of how the question is phrased. Identify exactly what information you need to find in the passage. Search the question for terms that will guide you to the pertinent passage in the text.
2. **Use Context Clues**: Once you locate the relevant part of the passage, read the surrounding sentences to understand the context. This will help you accurately interpret the specific detail being questioned.
3. **Emphasize or Highlight Important Details**: Underline or highlight significant elements in the passage, such as names, dates, locations, and particular examples. Finding the information will be simpler as a result, especially when responding to detailed queries.
4. **Eliminate Incorrect Options**: Reduce the number of options by using the process of elimination. Discard answers that are clearly incorrect or not mentioned in the passage. Pay attention to the choices that are directly related to the given information.
5. **Refer Back to the Passage**: Make sure your response is accurate by always consulting the passage. Make that the response you have selected appropriately captures the information provided and is backed up by the text.

Common Pitfalls and How to Avoid Them
- **Misinterpreting Information**: Specific detail questions require precise answers. Be careful not to misinterpret the information or make assumptions beyond what is stated in the passage. Stick closely to the text.
- **Overlooking Key Details**: It's easy to overlook small but crucial details when reading quickly. In order to make sure you don't miss any crucial information, engage in active reading strategies like annotating the passage.
- **Choosing Answers Based on General Knowledge**: You should only base your response on the facts in the passage; don't include any material from your past experiences or personal beliefs. Specific detail questions are about recalling or locating facts from the text.

Practice Questions
Example 1: "The Amazon rainforest, often referred to as the 'lungs of the Earth,' plays a critical role in regulating the global climate. It produces approximately 20% of the world's oxygen and is home to an incredibly diverse range of flora and fauna. However, deforestation poses a significant threat to this vital ecosystem, leading to loss of biodiversity and contributing to climate change."

Question: "According to the passage, what percentage of the world's oxygen is produced by the Amazon rainforest?"

Answer: "Approximately 20%."

Example 2: "The first woman to receive the Nobel Prize in physics and chemistry, Marie Curie is still the sole recipient of the honor in two distinct scientific disciplines. Her seminal work on radioactivity opened the door to important developments in physics and medicine."

Question: "According to the passage, what is Marie Curie known for being the first woman to achieve?"

Answer: "The first woman to win a Nobel Prize."

Advanced Techniques
1. **Paraphrasing**: When searching for specific details, practice paraphrasing the question and the relevant text in your own words. This can aid in your comprehension and memory of the material.
2. **Understanding Implicit Details**: Some specific detail questions may require you to infer details that are not explicitly stated but are implied by the passage. Practice identifying these implicit details through careful reading and analysis.
3. **Recognizing Synonyms and Rephrasings**: The SAT® often rephrases details from the passage in the questions and answer choices. Be familiar with synonyms and different ways of expressing the same idea to avoid confusion.
4. **Timed Practice**: Practice answering specific detail questions under timed conditions. This will assist you in honing your ability to find and understand information rapidly, even in the tight time limitations of the exam.

You can do much better on the SAT® Reading and Writing portion by improving your ability to respond to targeted detail questions. To become skilled at finding and correctly interpreting the details that are necessary for providing an accurate response to these questions, practice frequently with a range of passages.

EVIDENCE-BASED QUESTIONS (TEXTUAL)

The SAT® Reading and Writing section includes evidence-based questions that measure a student's comprehension of a passage as well as their ability to pinpoint specific passages in the book that lend support to their interpretations and conclusions. This ability, which demonstrates a student's aptitude for critical and analytical thought about the material they read, is crucial for academic achievement.

Usually, there are two questions in an evidence-based question set. In the first question, students are asked about the paragraph's meaning or content. In the second, they are asked to pinpoint the precise section that provides evidence for the previous question's response. This style invites students to provide particular textual allusions to support their answers.

Example Passage: "In the wake of industrialization, the early 20th century saw a dramatic shift in labor practices. Workers, once confined to agrarian settings, flocked to burgeoning urban centers to take up jobs in factories. On the other hand, these new positions frequently required hard hours, unfavorable working conditions, and little pay. As a result, labor unions began to emerge, advocating for better pay, shorter working hours, and safer environments."

Example Question Pair:
What is the main reason workers moved to urban centers in the early 20th century?
Which of the following quotes from the passage best supports the answer to the previous question?
A) "Workers, once confined to agrarian settings, flocked to burgeoning urban centers."
B) "These new roles, however, often came with long hours, poor working conditions, and minimal wages."
C) "As a result, labor unions began to emerge."
D) "Advocating for better pay, shorter working hours, and safer environments."

Answer:
Workers moved to urban centers to take up jobs in factories.
A) "Workers, once confined to agrarian settings, flocked to burgeoning urban centers."

Strategies for Answering Evidence-Based Questions
1. **Read the First Question Carefully**: Understand what the first question is asking. Identify the main idea or specific detail it is inquiring about.
2. **Locate the Answer in the Passage**: Go back to the passage and find the section that best addresses the first question. Pay attention to keywords or phrases from the question that may be directly referenced in the text.
3. **Consider the Second Question**: Once you have an answer to the first question, read the second question, which asks you to identify supporting evidence. This question will often list several quotes or sections from the passage.
4. **Match Evidence to Answer**: Compare each option provided in the second question with the section of the text you believe answers the first question. Look for direct references or closely related information that supports your initial answer.
5. **Eliminate Incorrect Options**: Discard options that don't directly support your response to the first question by using the process of elimination. Be meticulous in ensuring that the evidence aligns with your understanding of the passage.

Common Pitfalls and How to Avoid Them
- **Misinterpreting the First Question**: Ensure you fully understand what the first question is asking before looking for evidence. Misinterpreting the question can lead you to select incorrect evidence.
- **Choosing Partial Evidence**: Sometimes an answer choice may seem partially correct but does not fully support the answer. Always select the most comprehensive and direct evidence.
- **Ignoring Context**: Evidence should be understood in the context of the passage. Reading surrounding sentences can provide clarity and prevent misunderstandings.

Advanced Techniques
- **Cross-Referencing Information**: Practice cross-referencing information within the passage. This can help you identify sections of the text that provide a fuller understanding of the context.
- **Highlighting and Annotating**: When practicing, highlight or annotate passages. Mark sections that seem important or that you think may be referenced in evidence-based questions.
- **Synthesizing Information**: Work on combining the material included in the passage's many sections. There are instances when answering evidence-based questions necessitates knowing the connections between various textual elements.

Practice Techniques
1. **Timed Practice**: Practice answering evidence-based questions under timed conditions. You'll be able to adjust to the exam's pace with the help of this.
2. **Multiple Passages**: Work with a variety of passages from different genres and subjects. Your capacity to recognize and comprehend evidence in a variety of circumstances will improve as a result.
3. **Peer Review**: Discuss passages and answers with peers. Explaining your reasoning and hearing others' perspectives can deepen your understanding and uncover new strategies.

You can improve your SAT® Reading and Writing score and gain critical analytical abilities that you can use in both academic and professional situations by becoming proficient with evidence-based questions. Practice frequently, concentrate on comprehending the context of the material, and hone your skills in locating explicit textual evidence for your responses.

EVIDENCE-BASED QUESTIONS (QUANTITATIVE)

The Digital SAT®'s evidence-based questions test students' analytical and reading comprehension abilities as well as their ability to comprehend and synthesize quantitative data. These tests are intended to assess a student's capacity to synthesize data from written texts with information from tables, charts, and graphs, indicating a comprehensive comprehension of the subject matter. This chapter will offer a thorough tutorial on how to approach these quantitative, evidence-based issues in an efficient manner.

In quantitative evidence-based inquiries, a passage or scenario is usually presented along with quantitative data in the form of graphs, tables, or charts. To correctly answer the following questions, the student must evaluate the information in connection with the passage. These tests evaluate the student's comprehension of statistical measurements, data interpretation, and textual context application of mathematical reasoning.

Example Passage and Data: "In recent years, the implementation of renewable energy sources has become a priority in many countries. A study conducted in 2021 highlighted the growth rates of solar and wind energy in five different countries. The table below shows the percentage increase in energy production from these sources between 2018 and 2021."

Country	Solar Energy Growth (%)	Wind Energy Growth (%)
Country A	35%	28%
Country B	42%	34%
Country C	25%	18%
Country D	30%	22%
Country E	50%	40%

Example Question Pair:
Which country experienced the highest overall increase in renewable energy production?
Which data point from the table best supports your answer to the previous question?
A) Country A: Solar 35%, Wind 28%
B) Country B: Solar 42%, Wind 34%
C) Country C: Solar 25%, Wind 18%
D) Country D: Solar 30%, Wind 22%
E) Country E: Solar 50%, Wind 40%

Answer:
Country E experienced the highest overall increase in renewable energy production.
E) Country E: Solar 50%, Wind 40%

Strategies for Answering Quantitative Evidence-Based Questions
1. **Understand the Context**: Begin by reading the passage to understand the context of the quantitative data. This will help you grasp the overall theme and purpose of the data presented.
2. **Analyze the Data**: Examine the chart, graph, or table provided. Note any trends, patterns, or significant figures that stand out. The labels, units, and legends should all be carefully observed because they include important information for interpretation.
3. **Correlate Data with Text**: Connect the quantitative data with the information in the passage. Identify how the data supports or elaborates on the points made in the text. This correlation is key to answering the questions accurately.
4. **Answer the First Question**: Focus on the first question and use your understanding of the passage and data to find the answer. Ensure that your answer is well-supported by the quantitative information provided.
5. **Find Supporting Evidence**: For the second question, identify the specific data point that best supports your answer to the first question. This often involves selecting the most relevant figures or trends that directly align with your interpretation of the passage.

Common Pitfalls and How to Avoid Them
- **Overlooking Data Details**: Students often miss crucial details in the data presentation. Always examine all parts of the chart or table, including titles, labels, and units, to ensure a comprehensive understanding.
- **Ignoring the Passage Context**: While the data is critical, it must be understood within the context of the passage. Ignoring the passage can lead to misinterpretation of the data. Always refer back to the text when analyzing the data.
- **Rushing Through Analysis**: Quantitative questions require careful analysis. Avoid rushing through the data interpretation. Make sure your responses are precise and accurate by taking your time.

Advanced Techniques
- **Cross-Referencing Information**: Practice cross-referencing information within the passage and data. This skill helps in understanding how different parts of the passage relate to the quantitative information provided.
- **Highlighting Key Data Points**: When practicing, highlight or annotate key data points that are likely to be relevant to questions. This facilitates finding and referring to these points during the test.
- **Understanding Statistical Measures**: Learn about common statistical metrics like range, mean, median, and mode. Gaining an understanding of these ideas can aid in more accurate data interpretation.

You will improve your SAT® Reading and Writing score as well as acquire critical skills for success in both your academic and professional endeavors by becoming proficient with quantitative evidence-based questions. You will perform much better on these kinds of problems if you practice frequently, concentrate on integrating textual and numeric information, and hone your critical data analysis skills

.

INTERFERENCE-BASE QUESTIONS

Students are challenged with Digital SAT® inference-based questions to deduce logical implications from given information, beyond the passage's clear content. These questions are intended to assess a student's comprehension of underlying themes, inferential reasoning, and the ability to read between the lines in a book. Because inference-based questions need sophisticated reading comprehension and critical thinking abilities, mastering them is crucial to getting good marks on the SAT® Reading and Writing portion.

There are no explicit responses to questions based on inferences in the text. Rather, in order to reach a conclusion, the reader must employ logical reasoning, apply past knowledge, and synthesize information from various sections of the paragraph. The opening statements of these queries frequently include "It can be inferred that," "The author implies that," or "Based on the passage, it is most likely that."

Example Passage: "In the early 20th century, urbanization and industrialization were rapidly transforming American cities. This era, marked by significant social and economic changes, saw a shift in the workforce from agrarian to industrial jobs. Many families moved from rural areas to urban centers in search of better employment opportunities, leading to the growth of cities. However, this transition was not without challenges. Inadequate public services, cramped living quarters, and labor unrest were prevalent as cities failed to keep up with the fast growth in population."

Example Question: It can be inferred from the passage that the rapid growth of cities in the early 20th century led to:
A) Improved living conditions for all residents.
B) Decreased opportunities for employment in rural areas.
C) Challenges related to overcrowding and public services.
D) A decrease in labor unrest due to better working conditions.

Answer: C) Challenges related to overcrowding and public services.

Strategies for Answering Inference-Based Questions

1. **Read the Passage Thoroughly**: Begin by carefully reading the passage to understand the main ideas and details. The text's tone, style, and organization should all be taken into consideration as they might offer crucial context for drawing conclusions.
2. **Identify Key Information**: Emphasize or highlight important details that are expressed clearly in the passage. This will assist you in recognizing the relationships between the text's various sections and locating the premises for any possible deductions.
3. **Consider the Author's Purpose**: Think about the author's intent and perspective. Understanding why the author wrote the passage and what they aim to convey can provide valuable clues for making inferences.
4. **Look for Contextual Clues**: Inference-based questions often rely on subtle hints within the text. Look for words and phrases that suggest relationships, contrasts, or implications, and use these as the foundation for your inferences.
5. **Apply Logical Reasoning**: Make connections between the various bits of information in the passage by applying logic. Consider how the details fit together to form a broader understanding of the topic.
6. **Eliminate Implausible Options**: Carefully evaluate each answer choice and eliminate those that are clearly inconsistent with the information provided in the passage. You can reduce the number of possibilities to the most likely conclusion by using this process of elimination.

Common Pitfalls and How to Avoid Them

- **Making Unsupported Assumptions**: Avoid making assumptions that are not supported by the passage. Stick to information that can be logically inferred from the text, rather than relying on outside knowledge or personal opinions.
- **Overlooking Context**: Inferences should be grounded in the context of the passage. Be mindful of the overall theme and purpose of the text, and ensure that your inferences align with these elements.
- **Misinterpreting Details**: Pay close attention to the specific details provided in the passage. Misinterpreting or overlooking key information can lead to incorrect inferences.

Advanced Techniques

- **Synthesis of Information**: Practice synthesizing information from multiple parts of the passage. This involves integrating various details to form a comprehensive understanding and draw well-supported inferences.
- **Understanding Implicit Relationships**: Work on recognizing implicit relationships within the text. These can include cause and effect, comparison and contrast, or the relationship between different ideas and events.
- **Contextual Vocabulary**: Enhance your vocabulary skills to better understand and interpret subtle nuances in the passage. Gaining a clear understanding of words and phrases will greatly enhance your capacity for accurate inference.

You will improve your analytical and critical reading abilities, which are necessary for success on the SAT® and other tests, by becoming proficient with inference-based problems. These questions ask for a thorough comprehension of the material as well as the capacity to evaluate the data that is offered. You can build the abilities required to succeed in this difficult SAT® Reading and Writing part by consistently practicing and applying the strategies described in this chapter.

CHAPTER 15: CRAFT AND STRUCTURE

CONTEXTUAL VOCABULARY QUESTIONS

The purpose of the Digital SAT®'s contextual vocabulary questions is to assess a student's comprehension of words and phrases as they are employed in a paragraph. These questions assess a student's vocabulary knowledge as well as their comprehension of the author's goal, context, and subtleties. Achieving a good reading section score on the SAT® requires mastery of these questions.

Students must interpret words in contextual vocabulary questions by using the surrounding text to determine their meaning. To do this, examine the sentence or paragraph in which the word appears and determine how its usage affects the meaning as a whole. Take the following sentence, for example:

"The enigmatic smile of the Mona Lisa has intrigued art enthusiasts for centuries."

If asked about the meaning of "enigmatic," a student must look at the context provided by the rest of the sentence. The smile is described as intriguing art enthusiasts, suggesting a sense of mystery or puzzlement. Hence, "enigmatic" can be understood as "mysterious."

Strategies for Tackling Contextual Vocabulary Questions

- **Read the Surrounding Text Carefully**: Before and after the word in question, read at least one phrase. This prevents misunderstandings based only on the current sentence and aids in grasping the larger context.
- **Identify Clues**: Look for synonyms, antonyms, examples, or explanations within the surrounding text. Words like "but," "however," "for example," and "such as" often signal important contextual clues.
- **Substitute the Word**: Determine whether the statement still makes sense by trying to substitute the word with a possible synonym. This technique helps in narrowing down the choices.
- **Eliminate Wrong Answers**: Sift through the options and eliminate those that are obviously inappropriate for the situation. This raises the likelihood that, among the remaining possibilities, you will choose the right response.
- **Understand Common Prefixes and Suffixes**: Knowledge of common prefixes, suffixes, and root words can help in deducing the meaning of unfamiliar words. For example, the prefix "un-" often indicates negation, as in "unlikely" or "unhappy."

Examples and Practice

To illustrate, let's examine a few sample questions:

Example 1: "The artist's use of vibrant colors and bold strokes imbued the painting with a sense of vitality and energy."
In this sentence, "imbued" is likely to mean:
a) Diminished
b) Saturated
c) Drained
d) Infused

Analyzing the context, the painting is described as having vitality and energy due to the artist's technique. Therefore, "imbued" is closest in meaning to "infused."

Example 2: "Despite the complexity of the task, she tackled it with alacrity, surprising her colleagues with her enthusiasm."
Here, "alacrity" is likely to mean:
a) Reluctance
b) Indifference
c) Hesitation
d) Eagerness

Given that her approach surprised her colleagues positively, "alacrity" aligns best with "eagerness."

A large vocabulary comes in quite handy for these types of questions. It is encouraged of students to read widely and a variety of books. Learning new words on a regular basis in a variety of settings facilitates internalizing their definitions and applications.

In a text, words frequently have connotations that influence their meaning. It is important to know if a word has a neutral, positive, or negative meaning. When referring to children, for instance, the terms "childlike" and "childish" have different meanings; the former is typically good and suggests innocence, while the latter is negative and suggests immaturity. Let's consider another example:

"The politician's speech was filled with platitudes, offering little substance to the discerning audience."

Here, "platitudes" has a negative connotation, indicating that the speech was unoriginal or clichéd, providing little real value.

Learning how to answer questions with contextual vocabulary requires practice on practice exams. They support students in becoming accustomed to the format, question types, and time management of tests. Examining responses and recognizing errors are essential steps towards enhancing performance.

Questions involving contextual vocabulary may be especially difficult for non-native English speakers. It is imperative that they become fully immersed in English through a variety of media, such as books, articles, and audiovisual materials. A fuller knowledge of how words function in various settings can also be gained by concentrating on idiomatic expressions and colloquial usage.

Developing Analytical Skills

Analytical abilities are also tested by contextual vocabulary questions. Not only must students evaluate individual words, but also the connections between words and the passage overall. This entails figuring out the author's intent as well as trends and themes. Students can benefit from analytical reading tasks where they examine the word choice in essays or brief sections.

Sometimes, the tone or intention of the author strongly influences the meaning of a word or phrase. Determining the author's tone might help you understand the meaning of certain phrases, whether they are serious, amusing, critical, or sarcastic. For example:

"The scientist's groundbreaking theory, initially met with skepticism, eventually garnered accolades and recognition."

Here, "groundbreaking" indicates that the theory was innovative and significant, as suggested by the eventual recognition it received.

Students often fall into the trap of selecting words that fit the sentence grammatically but not contextually. It's essential to ensure that the chosen word not only makes sense within the sentence but also aligns with the overall meaning of the passage.

Example 3: "Her laconic responses during the interview did not reveal much about her personality."
"Laconic" in this context means:
a) Lengthy
b) Terse
c) Incoherent
d) Enthusiastic

Given that her responses did not reveal much, "laconic" most appropriately means "terse," or brief and to the point.

A combination of contextual comprehension and vocabulary knowledge is needed to answer contextual vocabulary questions. Constant practice can greatly improve performance, as can making an active effort to increase one's vocabulary and grasp linguistic nuances. Students can tackle these issues with more assurance and accuracy by incorporating these techniques into their study regimen.

It is crucial to comprehend the subtleties of the contextual vocabulary questions on the Digital SAT® in order to score highly. Students who practice these abilities will not only perform well on the SAT® but will also have a greater understanding of the complexity and depth of the English language.

PURPOSE-DRIVER QUESTIONS

Purpose-driven questions are an essential aspect of the Digital SAT® that evaluates a student's comprehension of the author's intention and the underlying purpose of particular textual pieces. These questions force students to read the material more closely and go beyond simple understanding to consider the author's intentions and goals. To score highly on the reading and writing portions of the SAT®, one must know how to approach purpose-driven questions.

Purpose-driven inquiries center on the rationale behind the author's decisions to use particular literary devices, incorporate particular details, or arrange the text in a particular way. These queries could focus on the passage's general goal or the objectives of certain paragraphs, sentences, or phrases. Students must deduce the author's intentions from these and assess how different textual elements support these intentions.

For example, a purpose-driven question might ask:

- What is the primary purpose of the first paragraph?
- Why does the author mention a particular study or example?
- How does the author use a particular analogy or metaphor?

Strategies for Answering Purpose-Driven Questions

1. **Identify the Main Idea**: Before diving into the specific purpose-driven question, ensure you have a solid grasp of the main idea of the passage. Understanding the central theme or argument will help you infer the purpose of individual components.

2. **Analyze the Context**: Look at the context surrounding the specific part of the text in question. Consider how it fits into the broader structure and argument of the passage. This includes examining preceding and following sentences or paragraphs to understand the flow of ideas.

3. **Consider the Author's Tone and Style**: The tone and style of the writing can provide significant clues about the author's purpose. Is the tone persuasive, informative, critical, or descriptive? You can determine why the author included specific material by looking at the author's word choice and general style.

4. **Look for Signal Words**: Authors often use signal words or phrases to indicate their purpose. Words like "for example," "therefore," "in contrast," and "moreover" can signal explanations, conclusions, contrasts, and additions that are essential to understanding the author's intent.

5. **Think Like the Author**: Put yourself in the author's shoes. Consider why you would include certain details or structure the text in a particular way if you were the author. This perspective can help you understand the rationale behind the author's choices.

Example Analysis

To illustrate these strategies, let's consider an example passage and a related purpose-driven question:

Example Passage: "In recent years, urban farming has emerged as a viable solution to address food insecurity in densely populated cities. By converting vacant lots into productive green spaces, urban farmers are not only providing fresh produce to local communities but also fostering a sense of community and environmental stewardship."

Example Question: What is the primary purpose of the second sentence in the passage?

Analysis: The second sentence states: "By converting vacant lots into productive green spaces, urban farmers are not only providing fresh produce to local communities but also fostering a sense of community and environmental stewardship."

We must take into account this sentence's context inside the passage in order to ascertain its intended meaning. Urban gardening is discussed in the opening phrase as a potential remedy for food insecurity. The second phrase goes into more detail on how urban farming accomplishes this by emphasizing the advantages that go beyond simply producing food, like community development and environmental advantages. Thus, the second sentence's goal is to provide examples of urban farming's wider effects, which will support the first sentence's thesis.

Types of Purpose-Driven Questions

- **Purpose of Specific Details**: These questions ask why the author included a specific fact, statistic, or example. They require students to connect the detail to the overall argument or theme.
- **Purpose of Paragraphs**: These questions focus on the role of an entire paragraph within the passage. It is

crucial that students understand the role that each paragraph plays in shaping the argument or story.

- **Purpose of Literary Devices**: These questions involve analyzing the purpose of metaphors, analogies, rhetorical questions, and other literary devices. It's important to comprehend how these strategies strengthen the text's meaning or argumentative force.
- **Purpose of the Entire Passage**: Sometimes, questions will ask about the primary purpose of the whole passage. This requires a holistic understanding of the text and its objectives.

Practice Questions

Example 1: "The rapid advancements in artificial intelligence are transforming industries around the world. For instance, in healthcare, AI systems are now capable of diagnosing diseases with remarkable accuracy, sometimes even outperforming human doctors. This innovation in technology not only enhances patient outcomes but also lowers expenses and boosts productivity."

Question: What is the primary purpose of the third sentence in the passage?

Analysis: The third sentence states: "This technological leap not only improves patient outcomes but also reduces costs and increases efficiency." The purpose of this sentence is to emphasize the benefits of AI advancements in healthcare, supporting the claim made in the second sentence about AI's capabilities.

Example 2: "While renewable energy sources such as wind and solar power have gained significant attention, it is crucial not to overlook the potential of geothermal energy. Unlike solar and wind energy, which are dependent on the weather, geothermal energy is produced from the heat that exists within the Earth and provides a steady, sustainable energy source that may run continually."

Question: Why does the author mention solar and wind energy in the passage?

Analysis: The mention of solar and wind energy serves to contrast these more commonly discussed renewable energy sources with geothermal energy. By highlighting the limitations of solar and wind energy, the author underscores the advantages of geothermal energy as a more reliable and continuous source.

Enhancing Analytical Skills

Strong analytical abilities are necessary for pupils to do well on purpose-driven questions. This calls for regular practice with careful reading and critical thinking. Students should read a variety of books, consider the author's writing strategies, and consider the motivations behind different writing decisions.

A sophisticated comprehension of the material and the author's goals is necessary to answer purpose-driven questions on the Digital SAT®. Students can enhance their reading comprehension and analytical abilities, which are essential for success on the SAT® and in academic endeavors beyond the test, by becoming proficient with these questions. Students who practice regularly and apply the tactics discussed in this chapter will have the tools necessary to successfully complete purpose-driven questions and the reading and writing sections of the Digital SAT®.

CONNECTION QUESTIONS

The Digital SAT®'s connection questions test a student's capacity to recognize and explain the connections between concepts, ideas, and events in a passage. These tests are intended to assess a student's ability to apply knowledge, make conclusions, and follow a text's logic. To get good grades in the reading and writing portions, you must know how to answer these questions.

Connection questions can take many different forms. For example, they can challenge students to explain how one passage relates to another, how an idea presented early in the book influences content covered later, or how numerous details within the text support the author's main point of contention. Students must use critical thinking skills to consider the text's coherence, organization, and interactions between its many parts in response to these questions.

For instance, a connection question might ask:

- In what way does the data presented in paragraph 2 bolster the author's claim made in paragraph 5?
- What is the relationship between the example given in the third paragraph and the overall theme of the passage?
- How do the ideas presented in the introduction connect to the conclusion?

Strategies for Answering Connection Questions

1. **Identify Key Ideas**: Start by pinpointing the main ideas or arguments in the passage. Understanding the primary message will help you see how different parts of the text are interconnected.
2. **Look for Transitional Phrases**: Transitional words and phrases like "therefore," "in contrast," "furthermore," and "for example" signal connections between ideas. These can offer hints as to how various textual components connect to one another.
3. **Analyze the Structure**: Consider the overall structure of the passage. How does the author introduce, develop, and conclude their argument? You can better understand the relationships between various sections by outlining the structure.
4. **Synthesize Information**: Synthesis is the process of putting several textual components together to create a cohesive understanding. Practice synthesizing information from various parts of the passage to answer connection questions effectively.
5. **Contextual Reading**: Be conscious of the situation in which the information is provided. Context can provide significant insights into how different parts of the text relate to each other and support the author's purpose.

Example Analysis

Let's analyze an example passage and related connection questions to illustrate these strategies:

Example Passage: "Recent studies on urban green spaces have highlighted their importance in enhancing the quality of life in cities. These areas have many advantages, including lowering air pollution, encouraging physical exercise, and stimulating social connection. In a survey conducted by the Urban Planning Institute, 75% of respondents reported feeling more connected to their community after the introduction of a new park in their neighborhood."

Example Questions: How does the survey mentioned in the last sentence support the information presented in the first sentence?

What is the relationship between the benefits of urban green spaces listed in the second sentence and the survey results?

Analysis: The survey's findings, which offer factual proof that urban green areas improve people's quality of life, corroborate the information in the first phrase. The initial claim is reinforced by the survey's finding that 75% of respondents felt better connected to their community once a park was introduced. This finding illustrates a particular benefit of urban green spaces. There is evidence and illustration in the relationship between the benefits listed and the survey findings. Generally speaking, the advantages of urban green spaces include lowering air pollution, encouraging physical activity, and enhancing social contacts. The survey's findings offer hard data supporting these advantages, emphasizing the social side of feeling more a part of the community.

Types of Connection Questions

- **Textual Relationships**: These questions ask about the relationship between different parts of the text. Students might be asked to connect a claim in one paragraph with supporting evidence in another.
- **Logical Flow**: Questions that focus on the logical progression of ideas in the text. Students must understand how the author's argument develops and how different points build on each other.
- **Comparative Analysis**: These questions may ask you to contrast and compare several textual passages. For example, students could be asked how two examples given in different paragraphs illustrate the same point or different aspects of an argument.
- **Causal Relationships**: Questions that explore cause-and-effect relationships within the text. Students need to identify how one event or idea leads to another.

Practice Questions

Example 1: "While renewable energy sources such as wind and solar power have gained significant attention, it is crucial not to overlook the potential of geothermal energy. In contrast to solar and wind energy, which are dependent on the weather, geothermal energy, which is generated from the heat that exists within the Earth, offers a steady and sustainable energy source that may run continually. A case study in Iceland demonstrates how geothermal energy can supply a substantial portion of the nation's electricity needs."

Question: How does the case study in the last sentence relate to the information presented in the first two sentences?

Analysis: The case study in Iceland provides a concrete example that supports the claims made in the first two sentences. It illustrates the stability and sustainability of geothermal energy by showing its practical application in supplying electricity, thus reinforcing the argument that geothermal energy should not be overlooked in favor of other renewable sources.

Example 2:

"Technological advancements in the field of artificial intelligence have led to significant improvements in various industries. AI technologies are currently used in healthcare to help diagnose illnesses with amazing precision. Furthermore, self-driving automobiles are growing and more common in the automobile industry. These improvements reveal how AI has the ability to revolutionize plenty of fields."

Question: How does the information about AI in healthcare relate to the information about AI in the automotive industry?

Analysis: These facts demonstrate AI's wide range of applications and revolutionary potential. The examples from healthcare and the automotive industry serve to highlight how AI is revolutionizing multiple sectors, thereby supporting the overall argument about the impact of technological advancements in AI.

Enhancing Analytical Skills

Students who want to do well on connection questions need to practice critical reading and analysis on a regular basis. Students can get better at seeing and explaining connections within a passage by interacting with a variety of texts and using the above-mentioned tactics.

The Digital SAT®'s connection questions encourage students to comprehend and explain the connections between various textual elements. Students can enhance their reading comprehension and analytical skills, which are essential for success on the SAT® and other tests, by becoming proficient with these questions. Students will gain the skills needed to perform well on connection questions and receive high marks in the reading and writing portions of the Digital SAT® with consistent practice and a methodical approach to understanding text structures and links.

CHAPTER 16: ARTICULTION OF IEAS

SYNTHESIS QUERIES

In order to succeed in the reading and writing portions of the Digital SAT®, students must possess the critical ability to synthesize knowledge from many sources. Students' comprehension, analysis, and connecting skills are tested via synthesis questions, which call for the integration and comparison of data from several books. This chapter examines the nature of synthesis queries, discusses methods for answering them successfully, and presents real-world examples to improve comprehension and application.

Students are frequently asked to evaluate arguments, find similar themes, or make conclusions based on data from two or more sources in synthesis inquiry. The purpose of these questions is to assess students' critical thinking abilities as well as their capacity to apply knowledge in a variety of situations.

Key Characteristics of Synthesis Queries:

- **Multiple Sources**: Synthesis queries typically involve two or more passages or excerpts that present related information or contrasting viewpoints.
- **Integration of Information**: The primary task is to integrate information from these sources to answer questions that go beyond the content of a single passage.
- **Critical Analysis**: Students must analyze the relationships between the sources, including similarities, differences, and overarching themes.

Strategies for Tackling Synthesis Queries

1. **Read and Annotate Each Passage Separately**: Begin by reading each passage individually, making notes on the main ideas, arguments, and key points. This preliminary stage guarantees a comprehensive comprehension of every source prior to trying their synthesis.
2. **Identify Common Themes and Differences**: Look for recurring themes, arguments, or pieces of evidence across the passages. Identify points of agreement and contention between the sources. This step is crucial for answering questions that require a comparison or contrast of information.
3. **Use a Graphic Organizer**: Employing a graphic organizer, such as a Venn diagram or a comparison chart, can help visually map out the relationships between the passages. This tool aids in organizing thoughts and highlighting critical connections.
4. **Synthesize Before Answering**: Before answering the questions, take a moment to synthesize the information. Formulate a clear, coherent understanding of how the passages relate to each other. This mental synthesis ensures that your answers are well-informed and comprehensive.
5. **Refer Back to the Texts**: Always refer back to the texts when formulating your answers. Quotations, specific details, and direct references provide strong support for your responses and demonstrate a thorough engagement with the material.

Practical Examples of Synthesis Queries

To illustrate the application of these strategies, let's consider a synthesis query involving two passages about climate change.

Passage 1: "Climate change, driven primarily by human activities such as the burning of fossil fuels and deforestation, has led to a significant increase in global temperatures. The effects of this warming are evident in the melting polar ice caps, rising sea levels, and increased frequency of extreme weather events. To lessen these effects and switch to sustainable energy sources, quick action is needed."

Passage 2: "While climate change presents a severe threat to the environment, it also offers an opportunity for innovation and economic growth. The shift towards renewable energy and green technologies has the potential to create jobs, reduce energy costs, and enhance energy security. The imperative to address environmental issues and the requirement to promote economic growth must be balanced by policymakers."

Example Synthesis Query: "Compare the perspectives of the two passages on the impacts of climate change and the proposed solutions. How do the authors' views align and diverge?"

Analysis:

- **Common Themes**: The serious threat that climate change poses is acknowledged in both paragraphs, as is the urgency of taking prompt action.
- **Divergent Views**: Passage 1 focuses primarily on the environmental impacts and the necessity of reducing fossil fuel consumption. Passage 2, while recognizing the threat, emphasizes the economic opportunities and benefits of transitioning to renewable energy.
- **Synthesis**: The synthesized answer should address the shared urgency for action while highlighting the different focal points—environmental conservation in Passage 1 and economic innovation in Passage 2.

Advanced Synthesis Techniques

- **Thematic Synthesis**: For queries requiring thematic synthesis, identify overarching themes that connect the passages. Discuss how each source contributes to the understanding of these themes, providing specific examples and evidence.
- **Comparative Analysis**: When comparing sources, discuss not only the similarities and differences but also the implications of these comparisons. Analyze how different perspectives enhance or challenge the overall understanding of the topic.
- **Evaluative Synthesis**: Evaluative synthesis goes a step further by assessing the strengths and weaknesses of each source. Critically evaluate the arguments presented, considering the evidence and reasoning used by the authors.

Practice Exercise

To solidify the understanding of synthesis queries, let's work through an exercise involving two new passages about technology in education.

Passage 1: "The integration of technology in education has revolutionized the learning experience. Students can now learn at their own pace and in accordance with their interests thanks to the availability of digital tools and resources that have made education more individualized and accessible. Still, a lot of students face the difficulty of the digital divide since they do not have access to the essential technology or internet connectivity."

Passage 2: "Technology in education offers numerous benefits, including interactive learning and access to vast amounts of information. However, an over emphasis on screen time and a decline in in-person engagement are two problems that might result from relying too much on digital tools. Teachers need to strike a balance between utilizing technology and sticking to their time-tested teaching strategies."

Synthesis Query: "Analyze how the two passages discuss the benefits and challenges of technology in education. What solutions do the authors propose to address the challenges mentioned?"

Analysis:

- **Benefits**: Both passages highlight the benefits of technology in making education more accessible and interactive.
- **Challenges**: Passage 1 discusses the digital divide, while Passage 2 addresses the potential negative impacts on face-to-face interaction and screen time.
- **Proposed Solutions**: Passage 1 suggests addressing the digital divide by improving access, whereas Passage 2 emphasizes finding a balance between digital and traditional methods.

To succeed in the reading and writing portions of the Digital SAT®, one must master synthesis queries. Students can exhibit critical thinking abilities and gain a deeper understanding of complicated subjects by learning how to combine information from many sources. Students will be better equipped to handle these difficult questions by practicing and using sophisticated synthesis strategies, which will ultimately result in greater performance and higher results.

TRANSITION QUERIES

The foundation of coherent and clear communication in academic reading and writing is the ability to recognize and use transitions successfully. The Digital SAT® includes transition questions to assess students' ability to identify and use transitional phrases and sentences that support a logical flow of ideas. This chapter analyzes the nature of transition inquiries, looks at different kinds of transitions, and offers tips and techniques for becoming proficient with them. Students are frequently asked to choose the best word, phrase, or sentence to connect ideas in a paragraph by answering transitional questions. These questions measure the student's capacity to write coherently and cohesively, guaranteeing a smooth and logical flow of ideas.

Key Characteristics of Transition Queries:
- **Contextual Relevance**: Transition queries are embedded within the context of a passage, requiring a deep understanding of the surrounding sentences and paragraphs.
- **Logical Flow**: The primary goal is to ensure that the chosen transition maintains the logical progression of ideas, whether it is introducing, contrasting, adding, or concluding points.
- **Types of Transitions**: Various types of transitions include additive (also, furthermore), adversative (however, on the other hand), causal (therefore, because), and sequential (first, next).

Types of Transitions
- **Additive Transitions**: Additive transitions are used to introduce additional information or reinforce previously mentioned points. Examples include: also, furthermore, moreover, in addition, and similarly.
  - *Example*: "The research highlights the benefits of a plant-based diet. Furthermore, it emphasizes the positive environmental impact of reducing meat consumption."
- **Adversative Transitions**: Adversative transitions highlight contrast or opposition between ideas. Common examples are: however, on the other hand, although, nevertheless, and conversely.
  - *Example*: "The initial results were promising. However, further testing revealed significant limitations in the methodology."
- **Causal Transitions**: Causal transitions indicate cause-and-effect relationships. Examples include: therefore, consequently, because, thus, and hence.
  - *Example*: "The company implemented new safety protocols. Consequently, workplace accidents have decreased significantly."
- **Sequential Transitions**: Sequential transitions indicate the order of events or steps in a process. Common examples are: first, next, then, finally, and subsequently.
  - *Example*: "First, gather all necessary materials. Next, follow the instructions carefully. Finally, review the results for accuracy."

Strategies for Tackling Transition Queries
1. **Understand the Context**: Before selecting a transition, carefully read the surrounding sentences and paragraphs to grasp the context fully. Understanding the relationship between ideas is crucial for choosing the correct transition.
2. **Identify the Purpose of the Transition**: Determine what the transition is intended to achieve. Is it illustrating a sequence, providing context, contrasting ideas, or demonstrating cause and effect? Recognizing the purpose helps narrow down the options.
3. **Eliminate Incorrect Choices**: Use the process of elimination to discard transitions that do not fit the context or disrupt the logical flow of ideas. This strategy increases the likelihood of selecting the correct transition.
4. **Read the Passage with the Transition**: After selecting a transition, read the passage with it in place to ensure it maintains coherence and enhances the logical progression of ideas.

Practical Examples of Transition Queries

To illustrate the application of these strategies, let's consider a transition query involving a passage about renewable energy.

Passage: "Renewable energy sources, such as solar and wind power, are becoming increasingly popular due to their environmental benefits. (1)___, they are not without their challenges. One major issue is the intermittent nature of these energy sources, which can lead to unreliable power supply."

Query: Which transition word or phrase best fits in the blank?

A. Furthermore

B. However

C. Consequently

D. For example

Analysis:

- **Context**: The text talks about the advantages and difficulties of renewable energy.
- **Purpose**: The blank is meant to introduce a contrasting point about the challenges.
- **Elimination**: "Furthermore" and "for example" add information, but do not indicate contrast. "Consequently" suggests a cause-and-effect relationship.
- **Correct Choice**: "However" is the best fit as it introduces a contrasting point.

Revised Passage: "Renewable energy sources, such as solar and wind power, are becoming increasingly popular due to their environmental benefits. However, they are not without their challenges. One major issue is the intermittent nature of these energy sources, which can lead to unreliable power supply."

Advanced Transition Techniques

- **Transitional Sentences**: In addition to single words or phrases, transitional sentences can bridge larger sections of text, providing a more comprehensive connection between ideas.
  - *Example*: "The initial phase of the project was completed on time. This achievement laid a strong foundation for the subsequent stages, ensuring that the team could proceed with confidence."
- **Parallel Structure**: Using parallel structure in transitions can enhance readability and emphasize the relationship between ideas.
  - *Example*: "Not only does exercise improve physical health, but it also boosts mental well-being. Similarly, a balanced diet contributes to overall health by providing essential nutrients."
- **Varying Transition Types**: Combining various transition styles together can make a passage's thoughts flow more naturally and captivatingly.
  - *Example*: "Renewable energy is cost-effective in the long run. Nevertheless, the initial investment can be substantial. Consequently, many governments offer incentives to encourage adoption. Moreover, technological advancements are gradually reducing these costs."

Practice Exercise

To solidify the understanding of transition queries, let's work through an exercise involving a passage about urban development.

Passage: "Urban development has led to significant economic growth in many cities. (1), it has also resulted in the displacement of low-income communities. (2), policymakers must balance growth with social equity to ensure inclusive development."

Queries:

Which transition word or phrase best fits in the blank (1)?

A. For instance

B. In addition

C. On the other hand

D. Therefore

Which transition word or phrase best fits in the blank (2)?
A. Consequently
B. Similarly
C. As a result
D. Furthermore

Analysis:
Blank (1):

- Context: The sentence contrasts economic growth with the displacement of communities.
- Purpose: To indicate contrast.
- Correct Choice: C. On the other hand

Blank (2):

- Context: The sentence introduces a need for balancing growth with equity.
- Purpose: To show cause and effect.
- Correct Choice: A. Consequently

Revised Passage: "Urban development has led to significant economic growth in many cities. On the other hand, it has also resulted in the displacement of low-income communities. Consequently, policymakers must balance growth with social equity to ensure inclusive development."

Gaining proficiency with transition queries is crucial for success in the Digital SAT®'s reading and writing sections. Students can improve their writing's coherence and cohesiveness and score higher on the test by learning to identify and utilize different kinds of transitions. Students will be well-prepared to take on these difficult problems by practicing and using advanced transition strategies, showcasing their skill in clearly expressing ideas.

CHAPTER 17: STANDARD ENGLISH CONVENTIONS

BASIC SENTENCE STRUCTURE

The ability to write well in English requires a solid understanding of sentence structure. Precise and convincing communication of ideas requires a thorough grasp of sentence structure and the functions of its components. This chapter will examine the basic elements of sentence structure, the range of sentence forms, and the typical mistakes that students should steer clear of in order to produce writing that is coherent and clear.

The subject, the predicate, and, frequently, further elements like objects, complements, and modifiers are the fundamental parts of a well-formed sentence. Every single one of these elements has a specific purpose in conveying the overall meaning of the sentence.

1. The Subject: The person, location, object, or idea that is carrying out the activity or being described is the subject of the sentence.

> *Example*: "The cat" in "The cat sleeps on the mat."

2. The Predicate: The verb is in the predicate, which also gives details about the subject's actions and circumstances.

> *Example*: "sleeps on the mat" in "The cat sleeps on the mat."

3. Objects: The verb's action is received by objects, which may be direct or indirect. A direct object answers the question "what?" or "whom?" after the verb, while an indirect object answers "to whom?" or "for whom?" the action is done.

> *Example*: Direct Object: "cake" in "She eats cake." Indirect Object: "him" in "She gave him a gift."

4. Complements: Complements add information about the subject or object. They can be subject complements (which rename or describe the subject) or object complements (which rename or describe the object).

> *Example*: Subject Complement: "a teacher" in "She is a teacher." Object Complement: "happy" in "The news made him happy."

5. Modifiers: Words, phrases, or clauses that give further information about one or more sentence elements are known as modifiers. Adjectives, adverbs, and more intricate phrases and clauses can be among them.

> *Example*: Adjective: "red" in "The red ball." Adverb: "quickly" in "She runs quickly."

Types of Sentences

Sentences can be divided into groups according to their composition and function. Knowing these categories makes it easier to change up sentence structures and produce work that is more interesting and lively.

1. Simple Sentences: A simple sentence contains one independent clause with a subject and a predicate.

> *Example*: "The dog barked."

2. Compound Sentences: When two or more separate sentences are connected by a semicolon or coordinating conjunction (for, and, nor, but, or, still, so), the sentence is considered compound.

> *Example*: "The sun set, and the stars appeared."

3. Complex Sentences: A complex sentence has a minimum of one dependent (subordinate) clause and one independent clause. Dependent clauses provide additional information but cannot stand alone as complete sentences.
Example: "Although it was raining, we went for a walk."

4. Compound-Complex Sentences: The components of both compound and complex sentences are combined in a compound-complex sentence. It has one or more dependent clauses together with a minimum of two independent clauses.
Example: "She completed her assignment, but she forgot to submit it because she was in a hurry."

Avoiding Common Pitfalls

Mastering sentence structure involves recognizing and avoiding common errors that can undermine clarity and coherence in writing. Some frequent pitfalls include fragments, run-on sentences, and comma splices.

1. Sentence Fragments: A sentence without a subject, predicate, or both is called a fragment.

> *Example of a Fragment*: "Running through the park."
> *Revised Sentence*: "She was running through the park."

2. Run-On Sentences: When two or more separate clauses are connected without the appropriate conjunction or punctuation, the sentence becomes run-on.

Example of a Run-On: "The weather was bad we stayed inside."
Revised Sentence: "The weather was bad, so we stayed inside."

3. Comma Splices: A comma splice happens when two independent clauses are incorrectly joined by a comma without a coordinating conjunction.
Example of a Comma Splice: "She loves to read, she spends hours at the library."
Revised Sentence: "She loves to read, and she spends hours at the library."

It's critical to employ a range of sentence forms in order to produce writing that is interesting and dynamic. Adding a mix of simple, compound, complex, and compound-complex sentences can make the material easier to read and more engaging. *Example of Sentence Variety:* Simple: "The dog barked." Compound: "The dog barked, and the cat hissed." Complex: "When the dog barked, the cat hissed." Compound-Complex: "When the dog barked, the cat hissed, and the bird flew away."

Practical Application
Let's apply these principles to a sample passage. Consider the following basic sentences:
"The student studied hard. She wanted to pass the exam. The exam was difficult."
By varying the sentence structure, we can create a more engaging passage:
"The student studied hard because she wanted to pass the difficult exam. Despite her efforts, the exam was challenging."

Diagramming Sentences
One effective method for understanding and mastering sentence structure is sentence diagramming. Diagramming involves visually breaking down a sentence into its component parts to see how each element functions and relates to others.
Example: Examine the phrase in question "The quick brown fox jumps over the lazy dog."
Diagram:

- **Subject**: "The quick brown fox"
- **Verb**: "jumps"
- **Prepositional Phrase**: "over the lazy dog"
- **Object of the Preposition**: "dog"

Exercises for Mastery
To reinforce the understanding of basic sentence structure, consider practicing with the following exercises:
1. Identify the Elements: Identify the subject, predicate, and objects in each sentence.
Example: "The teacher explained the lesson."

- **Subject**: "The teacher"
- **Predicate**: "explained"
- **Object**: "the lesson"

2. Combine Sentences: Construct compound or complicated sentences by combining the following simple sentences.
Example: "She opened the book. She began to read."
Combined: "She opened the book and began to read."
3. Correct the Errors: Identify and correct fragments, run-ons, and comma splices in the following sentences.
Example: "He enjoys hiking he often goes to the mountains."
Corrected: "He enjoys hiking; he often goes to the mountains."

Students can enhance their writing abilities and ensure that their thoughts are presented properly by learning the fundamentals of sentence construction. This basic understanding will act as a cornerstone for more complex writing standards and strategies that are discussed in later chapters.

PUNCTUATION: COMMAS, DASHES AND COLONS

In written language, punctuation marks serve as silent guides, highlighting meaning and establishing textual flow. Commas, dashes, and colons are important examples of these. They can significantly increase the impact and clarity of your work when applied appropriately. To help you become proficient with these crucial punctuation marks, this chapter will go into great detail about the conventions and subtleties of employing colons, dashes, and commas.

Commas

Commas are perhaps the most versatile and frequently used punctuation marks. They can be used to separate elements in a sentence, clarify meaning, and enhance readability. Here are the primary rules for using commas:

1. Separating Items in a Series: Commas are used to separate three or more items in a series.

Example: "She bought apples, oranges, bananas, and grapes."

2. Setting Off Introductory Elements: When introducing words, phrases, or clauses come before the main clause, place a comma after them.

Example: "After the meeting, we went out for lunch."

3. Before Coordinating Conjunctions in Compound Sentences: When a coordinating conjunction (for, and, nor, but, or, yet, so) links two separate clauses, use a comma before it.

Example: "I wanted to go to the concert, but I had to study for the exam."

4. Setting Off Nonessential Information: To distinguish between clauses, phrases, and words that are not vital to the sentence's primary idea, use commas.

Example: "My brother, who lives in New York, is visiting us next week."

5. Separating Adjectives: A comma should be used to separate adjectives that modify a noun equally, such as two or more.

Example: "It was a long, tiring day."

6. Direct Address: Use commas to set off the name or title of a person directly addressed.

Example: "Lisa, can you help me with this?"

7. Dates, Addresses, and Titles: Commas are used to separate elements in dates, addresses, and titles.

Example: "He was born on July 4, 1776, in Philadelphia, Pennsylvania."

Dashes

Dashes are used to emphasize or set off information by creating a dramatic break in the sentence's structure. The en dash (–) and the em dash (—) are the two primary forms of dashes.

1. Em Dash (—): Because of its versatility, the em dash can be used to highlight text, signal an interruption, and set off parenthetical information.

Example for Parenthetical Information: "My father—who is an excellent cook—prepared dinner last night."

Example for Emphasis: "There was only one thing he wanted—revenge."

Example for Interruption: "I was going to tell you—but never mind."

2. En Dash (–): The en dash is primarily used to indicate ranges or connections between things.

Example for Ranges: "The meeting is scheduled for 3:00–4:00 p.m."

Example for Connections: "The New York–Boston train leaves at noon."

Colons

Colons are used to introduce lists, quotations, explanations, or to emphasize a particular point. Their correct use can add clarity and impact to your writing.

1. Introducing Lists: When starting a list, use a colon, particularly if it comes after an independent sentence.

Example: "You will need the following items: a pencil, a notebook, and an eraser."

2. Introducing Quotations: Use A quotation should come after an independent clause and be preceded by a colon.

Example: "He said it best: 'To be or not to be, that is the question.'"

3. Introducing Explanations or Examples: To begin an explanation or an example pertaining to the previous clause, use a colon.

Example: "She had only one wish: to see her family again."

4. Emphasizing Information: A colon can be used to emphasize a particular piece of information that follows an independent clause.

Example: "There is one thing you must remember: always be yourself."

Practical Application

To fully understand the use of commas, dashes, and colons, let's apply these rules to a sample passage:

Original Passage: "The committee discussed several issues budget cuts employee benefits and the new project proposal. After a long debate the decision was made to delay the project. The director who is rarely in the office today was present to cast the deciding vote."

Revised Passage: "The committee discussed several issues: budget cuts, employee benefits, and the new project proposal. After a long debate, the decision was made to delay the project. The director—who is rarely in the office today—was present to cast the deciding vote."

Common Mistakes and How to Avoid Them

1. Misplaced Commas: The placement of commas can alter a sentence's meaning or lead to misunderstanding, so pay attention to where you put them.

Example of Misplaced Comma: "While eating, my friend, called."

Corrected: "While eating, my friend called."

2. Overusing Em Dashes: Em dashes are powerful but should be used sparingly to avoid making the text appear disjointed.

Example of Overuse: "The movie—though long—was exciting—and full of suspense."

Revised: "The movie, though long, was exciting and full of suspense."

3. Incorrect Use of Colons: Ensure that what precedes a colon is an independent clause.

Example of Incorrect Use: "She loves: reading, writing, and drawing."

Corrected: "She loves the following activities: reading, writing, and drawing."

Exercises for Mastery

To reinforce the understanding of commas, dashes, and colons, consider practicing with the following exercises:

- Punctuate the Sentences: Insert commas, dashes, and colons where appropriate.
  Example: "The concert scheduled for Friday has been postponed."
  Revised: "The concert—scheduled for Friday—has been postponed."

- **Identify and Correct Errors**: Review sentences to find and correct punctuation errors.
  Example: "My brother who is an engineer lives in Chicago."
  Corrected: "My brother, who is an engineer, lives in Chicago."

- **Rewrite the Passage**: Rewrite a given passage to correct punctuation and improve clarity.
  Example: "The list includes apples oranges and bananas. She said 'I will be late'."
  Revised: "The list includes: apples, oranges, and bananas. She said: 'I will be late.'"

By learning how to use commas, dashes, and colons correctly, students can improve the readability and impact of their work significantly. When used appropriately, these punctuation marks improve readability and guarantee that the intended meaning is clearly and convincingly communicated.

VERB AGREEMENT

Skill in verb agreement is essential for writing effectively. It guarantees that sentences are cohesive and grammatically sound. Verb agreement, often called subject-verb agreement, is the understanding that exists between a verb and its subject about person and number. The fundamentals of verb agreement, typical problems, and error-prevention techniques will all be covered in this chapter.

Fundamentally, verb agreement involves making sure the verb is the same number and person as the subject. The following are the basic guidelines:

- Plural subjects take verbs that are plural, whereas singular subjects take verbs that are singular..
  Examples:
  The cat runs swiftly. (singular subject and singular verb)
  The cats run swiftly. (plural subject and plural verb)
- 'And' joins compound subjects, which are usually plural and require a plural verb.
  Example:
  The teacher and the student discuss the lesson. (compound subject with a plural verb)
- In compound subjects connected by 'or' or 'nor,' the verb agrees with the subject's closest part.
  Examples:
  Neither the teacher nor the students understand the assignment. (verb agrees with the plural noun 'students')
  Either the students or the teacher understands the assignment. (verb agrees with the singular noun 'teacher')

Special Cases in Verb Agreement

While the basic principles cover most situations, several special cases can complicate verb agreement. Let's explore some of these:

- **Collective Nouns**: Nouns that describe a group, such "team," "jury," "family," etc., can have a singular or plural verb depending on whether the group functions as a single entity or as separate entities.
  Examples:
  The team is winning. (acting as a single unit)
  The team are arguing among themselves. (acting as individuals)
- **Indefinite Pronouns**: Indefinite pronouns, like 'everyone,' 'someone,' 'nobody,' etc., are singular and take singular verbs.
  Examples:
  Everyone is invited to the party.
  Somebody knows the answer.
- **Nouns with Plural Forms but Singular Meanings**: Some nouns, such as 'news,' 'mathematics,' and 'physics,' appear plural but are singular and take singular verbs.
  Examples:
  The news is on at 6 PM.
  Mathematics is my favorite subject.
- **Subjects Separated from Verbs**: Be cautious of phrases that separate the subject from the verb, potentially leading to agreement errors.
  Examples:
  The bouquet of roses smells delightful. (The subject 'bouquet' is singular, not 'roses')
  The quality of the photos is exceptional.

Complex Structures and Verb Agreement

In more complex sentence structures, maintaining proper verb agreement can be challenging. Here are some guidelines to manage such complexities:

- **Relative Clauses**: Make sure the verb in sentences with relative clauses (those starting with who, which, or that) agrees with the relative pronoun's antecedent.
  Examples:

She is one of the students who are going to the competition. ('students' is plural)
This is the only one of the cakes that has chocolate icing. ('one' is singular)

- **Inverted Sentences**: Make that the verb still agrees with the subject in phrases where the verb comes after the subject.
  Examples:
  There is a problem with the solution. (subject 'problem' is singular)
  Here are the results of the experiment. (subject 'results' is plural)
- **Titles and Quoted Phrases**: Titles of works and quoted phrases take singular verbs, even if they contain plural nouns.
  Examples:
  "The Grapes of Wrath" is a classic novel.
  "Friends and Family" is a popular TV show segment.

Troubleshooting Common Verb Agreement Errors
Even experienced writers can struggle with verb agreement, especially in complex sentences. Here are some common errors and tips to avoid them:

- **Ignoring the Subject in Prepositional Phrases**: Writers often mistakenly let the noun in a prepositional phrase affect verb agreement. Instead of agreeing with the preposition's object, the verb should do so with the subject.
  Examples:
  The list of items is on the table. (subject 'list' is singular)
  A bouquet of flowers was given to her. (subject 'bouquet' is singular)
- **Misidentifying the Subject**: Ensure you correctly identify the subject, especially in lengthy or complex sentences.
  Examples:
  One of the students is absent. (subject 'one' is singular)
  Each of the players has a unique strategy. (subject 'each' is singular)
- **Agreement with Indefinite Pronouns**: There are a lot of singular indefinite pronouns that belong with single verbs.
  Examples:
  Everybody loves the new movie.
  Everything is set for the presentation.

Practice with Examples
Let's solidify our understanding of verb agreement with practical examples:

Correct the Verb Agreement:
The group of students (is/are) planning a trip.
The data (was/were) analyzed thoroughly.
Neither the manager nor the employees (has/have) arrived.
Answers:
The group of students is planning a trip.
The data were analyzed thoroughly.
Neither the manager nor the employees have arrived.

Choose the Correct Verb:
Each of the answers (is/are) correct.
The committee (disagree/disagrees) on the new policy.
Either my mother or my sisters (is/are) going to bake the cake.
Answers:
Each of the answers is correct.
The committee disagrees on the new policy.
Either my mother or my sisters are going to bake the cake.

Application in Writing
Using verb agreement correctly improves the writing's clarity and professionalism. Consider the following passage, initially containing verb agreement errors, and then corrected for proper agreement:

Original Passage: The students in the class enjoys the new curriculum. Each of the teachers have their own teaching style, but the results speaks for itself. The committee on curriculum changes meet every month.

Corrected Passage: The students in the class enjoy the new curriculum. Each of the teachers has their own teaching style, but the results speak for themselves. The committee on curriculum changes meets every month.

PRONOUN AGREEMENT

Comprehension and utilization of pronoun agreement are essential for writing that is both clear and efficient. Pronoun agreement makes ensuring that the number and gender of pronouns match the nouns they replace. The fundamentals of pronoun agreement, typical problems, and techniques for preserving agreement in complicated sentences will all be covered in this chapter.

Pronoun agreement essentially refers to matching a pronoun's number, gender, and person to that of its antecedent, or the noun it substitutes. Here are the fundamental rules:

- Plural pronouns belong with plural nouns, and single pronouns with singular nouns.
  Examples:
  The student lost her book. (singular noun 'student' and singular pronoun 'her')
  The students lost their books. (plural noun 'students' and plural pronoun 'their')

- Pronouns and the nouns they replace need to match in gender.
  Examples:
  John finished his homework. (masculine noun 'John' and masculine pronoun 'his')
  Mary finished her homework. (feminine noun 'Mary' and feminine pronoun 'her')

- Pronouns and the nouns they replace need to get along in person.
  Examples:
  I completed my assignment. (first person singular noun 'I' and first person singular pronoun 'my')
  You completed your assignment. (second person singular/plural noun 'you' and second person singular/plural pronoun 'your')

Common Challenges in Pronoun Agreement
While the basic principles cover most situations, several common challenges can complicate pronoun agreement. Let's explore some of these:

- **Collective Nouns**: The singular or plural form of collective nouns, such as "team," "jury," "family," etc., depends on whether the group functions as a single entity or as separate people.
  Examples:
  The team celebrated its victory. (acting as a single unit)
  The team put on their uniforms. (acting as individuals)

- **Indefinite Pronouns:** Pronouns that are indefinite, like "everyone," "someone," "nobody," etc., are often single and accept other singular pronouns.
  Examples:
  Everyone should bring his or her own lunch.
  Someone left his or her bag in the classroom.
  Note: While the singular 'they' is increasingly accepted to avoid gender-specific pronouns, it is essential to maintain traditional agreement in formal writing.

- **Compound Antecedents**: If a pronoun is used to indicate compound antecedents that are connected by 'and,' it has to be plural. The pronoun must line up with the closest antecedent when joined by "or" or "nor."
  Examples:
  Sarah and Tom said they would come. (plural pronoun 'they')
  Neither the manager nor the employees had their report ready. (plural pronoun 'their')
  Either the teacher or the students will present their projects. (plural pronoun 'their' agreeing with 'students')

- **Ambiguous Antecedents**: Avoid ambiguity by ensuring it is clear which noun a pronoun is replacing.
  Examples:
  Ambiguous: When Jane asked Mary, she was unsure. (Unclear who 'she' refers to)
  Clear: Jane was unsure when she asked Mary.

Troubleshooting Common Pronoun Agreement Errors

Even experienced writers can struggle with pronoun agreement, particularly in complex sentences. Here are some typical mistakes to watch out for:

- **Ignoring the Antecedent in Prepositional Phrases**: Ensure the pronoun agrees with the actual antecedent, not a noun within a prepositional phrase.
  Examples:
  The bouquet of flowers is beautiful in its vase. (antecedent 'bouquet' is singular)
  The group of students presented their project. (antecedent 'group' is singular in most contexts, but 'students' might make it plural depending on context)
- **Misidentifying the Antecedent**: Ensure you correctly identify the antecedent, especially in lengthy or complex sentences.
  Examples:
  Each of the players has his or her own strategy. (antecedent 'each' is singular)
  The members of the committee expressed their opinions. (antecedent 'members' is plural)
- **Agreement with Indefinite Pronouns**: There are a lot of singular indefinite pronouns that need to be paired with other singular pronouns.
  Examples:
  Everybody needs to bring his or her identification. (or 'their' in more casual or modern usage)
  Each of the answers is correct in its context.

Practice with Examples

Let's solidify our understanding of pronoun agreement with practical examples:

Correct the Pronoun Agreement:
Each student must bring their own book.
Neither John nor his friends have completed his assignments.
Someone left their bag on the bus.
Answers:
Every student must bring his or her own book. (or 'their' in modern usage)
Neither John nor his friends have completed their assignments.
Someone left his or her bag on the bus. (or 'their' in modern usage)

Choose the Correct Pronoun:
Each of the employees has his or her/their own locker.
If anybody calls, tell him or her/them I am out.
The committee reached its/their decision.
Answers:
Each of the employees has his or her own locker. (or 'their' in modern usage)
If anybody calls, tell him or her I am out. (or 'them' in modern usage)
The committee reached its decision. (typically treated as singular)

Application in Writing

Pronoun agreement should be used effectively to improve writing's clarity and professionalism. Consider the following passage, initially containing pronoun agreement errors, and then corrected for proper agreement:
Original Passage: Each of the students must submit their homework by Friday. If anyone has questions, they should ask the teacher. The committee finished their review, and it is pleased with the results.
Corrected Passage: Each of the students must submit his or her homework by Friday. If anyone has questions, he or she should ask the teacher. The committee finished its review, and it is pleased with the results.

MODIFIER AGREEMENT

A key component of grammar that guarantees written clarity and accuracy is modifier agreement. Adjectives, adverbs, and phrases that add details about a topic are examples of modifiers. Modifiers must make sense and have a clear relationship to the words they modify. Ambiguity and confusion may arise from improper modifier agreement maintenance. This chapter explores the fundamentals of modifier agreement, typical mistakes, and writing techniques for clarity. Modifiers have to be placed next to the words they are supposed to alter in order to avoid misunderstandings. Incorrect modifier placement frequently results in misplaced and dangling modifiers.

- **Misplaced Modifiers**: A misplaced modifier is a word, phrase, or clause that is improperly separated from the word it describes. This can make a sentence awkward and even unintentionally humorous.
  Examples:
  Misplaced: She almost drove her kids to school every day. (This suggests she didn't actually drive them.)
  Correct: She drove her kids to school almost every day. (This clarifies the frequency of the action.)

- **Dangling Modifiers**: When a modifier in a sentence is not made explicit, it becomes a dangling modifier. This often happens with introductory phrases.
  Examples:
  Dangling: Running to the bus stop, the rain began to fall. (It seems like the rain is running to the bus stop.)
  Correct: Running to the bus stop, I felt the rain begin to fall. (This clarifies that 'I' was running.)

Types of Modifiers and Their Placement
Modifiers can be single words, phrases, or clauses. Each type of modifier has specific rules for placement to ensure clarity.

- **Adjectives**: Adjectives modify nouns and pronouns, providing more information about them. They frequently follow linking verbs or come before the nouns they modify.
  Examples:
  Before a noun: The diligent student completed her assignment early.
  After a linking verb: The student was diligent.

- **Adverbs**: Adverbs generally describe how, when, where, or to what extent. They can also modify verbs, adjectives, or other adverbs.
  Examples:
  Modifying a verb: He quickly finished his homework.
  Modifying an adjective: She is extremely diligent.
  Modifying another adverb: He completed the task very quickly.

- **Adverbial Phrases and Clauses**: These provide additional information about the verb and typically need to be placed carefully to avoid ambiguity.
  Examples:
  Phrase: She completed her work on time, despite the challenges.
  Clause: Because she studied hard, she passed the exam with flying colors.

- **Participial Phrases**: These phrases function as adjectives and should be placed next to the noun or pronoun they modify.
  Examples:
  Correct: Exhausted from the long run, Jenna collapsed on the couch.
  Misplaced: Jenna collapsed on the couch, exhausted from the long run. (This can still be clear, but it's less direct.)

Ensuring Modifier Agreement
To achieve modifier agreement, follow these guidelines:

- **Place modifiers close to the words they modify**: Ensure that the modifier directly precedes or follows the word it describes to avoid confusion.
  Example:
  Misplaced: The teacher said on Monday she would return the tests.
  Correct: The teacher said she would return the tests on Monday.

- **Revise dangling modifiers**: Ensure the sentence includes the word being modified by the introductory phrase.

Example:
Dangling: After finishing the assignment, the TV was turned on.
Correct: After finishing the assignment, she turned on the TV.

- **Clarify ambiguous modifiers**: Reword sentences to remove any ambiguity caused by unclear modifier placement.
  Example:
  Ambiguous: She saw a man with a telescope.
  Clarified: With a telescope, she saw a man.
- **Avoid squinting modifiers**: These occur when a modifier could refer to either of two words, leading to confusion.
  Example:
  Squinting: Students who study rarely fail.
  Clarified: Students who study diligently rarely fail.

Practical Applications

Understanding and applying proper modifier agreement is essential in both academic writing and everyday communication. Here are a few strategies to ensure accuracy:

1. **Read sentences aloud**: It can be easier to see lost or dangling modifiers when reading aloud than when reading silently.
2. **Use peer review**: Get a second opinion on your writing to aid you discover any errors you may have missed. Problems with modifier placement are frequently visible to a new set of eyes.
3. **Practice with exercises**: Regular practice with exercises focused on modifier placement can help reinforce these rules.

Advanced Considerations

For those seeking to refine their writing further, consider these advanced aspects of modifier agreement:

- **Cumulative and Coordinate Adjectives**: Understand the difference between cumulative and coordinate adjectives, as their placement and punctuation differ.
  Examples:
  Cumulative: The big old house (no commas needed as the adjectives build on each other).
  Coordinate: The big, old house (commas needed as each adjective independently describes the noun).
- **Limiting Modifiers**: Pay attention to limiting modifiers such as 'only,' 'just,' 'almost,' and 'nearly,' which should be placed immediately before the word they modify to avoid ambiguity.
  Examples:
  Misplaced: She almost ate the entire cake.
  Correct: She ate almost the entire cake.
- **Disruptive Modifiers**: Be mindful of modifiers that can disrupt the flow of a sentence. While modifiers add detail, excessive or improperly placed modifiers can make sentences cumbersome.
  Examples:
  Disruptive: The book, which was on the table, that I wanted to read, was gone.
  Improved: The book that I wanted to read, which was on the table, was gone.

To sum up, mastering modifier agreement is necessary for communicating ideas clearly and effectively. Students can improve their clarity and precision, guaranteeing that their intended meaning is communicated without ambiguity, by comprehending and putting the rules of proper modifier placement into practice. Writing greatness can be attained with the help of meticulous editing, frequent practice, and a deep understanding of typical mistakes.

CHAPTER 18: ACCESSING 5 FULL-LENGTH PRACTICE TEST

One of the best ways to get ready for the Digital SAT® is to practice using full-length examinations on a regular basis. Taking into account this requirement, we have chosen five thorough practice exams that are accessible in PDF format. Although the real Digital SAT® is an adaptive test, there are several advantages to using practice exams in PDF format that are designed to replicate the exam environment. This chapter describes the benefits of using these PDF practice exams, how they mimic the examination environment, and how to get access to them.

Why Use PDF Practice Tests?
1. **Simulating the Testing Environment**: The Digital SAT® is a computer-based exam. Our PDF practice exams, however, are made to mimic the setup of the real test. By using these PDFs, students can get accustomed to the types of questions and the format they will encounter, allowing them to build confidence and reduce anxiety.
2. **Structured Practice Sessions**: Each of our practice tests is designed to be taken in a single sitting, mirroring the actual duration of the Digital SAT®. Students gain endurance from this and become accustomed to the time limits they would encounter on test day.
3. **Familiarization with Question Types**: The practice tests include a variety of question types found on the Digital SAT®, including multiple-choice, grid-in, and evidence-based reading and writing questions. This exposure helps students become comfortable with the different formats and improves their problem-solving skills.
4. **Self-Assessment:** A thorough answer key and explanations for every question are included in each PDF. Students are able to evaluate their performance, recognize their errors, and grow from them as a result. The ability to review answers and understand why certain choices are correct or incorrect is crucial for continuous improvement.
5. **Accessibility and Convenience**: The practice tests are easily accessible online. Students can download the PDFs to any device, print them out if they prefer, and complete them at their convenience. This flexibility ensures that students can integrate practice into their schedules without the need for specialized software or internet access during the test itself.

Access Full-Length Practice Tests
To provide the most realistic and convenient practice experience, our five full-length practice tests are available through easy online access. Here's how you can obtain and utilize these practice tests:
- **Clicking the Link**: You can access the practice tests by clicking on the provided link. This link will take you to a secure download page where you can obtain the PDFs. Each test is labeled and organized for easy navigation.
  https://drive.google.com/drive/folders/1BaZkah69MTYNKrgBodezabOAqhKedc8l?usp=sharing
- **Scanning the QR Code**: For even quicker access, scan the QR code provided below with your smartphone or tablet. This will direct you to the same download page, allowing you to save the practice tests directly to your device.

Download Here

- **Via Email**: If you encounter any difficulties downloading the tests, simply email us at **publishingltd@outlook.com** and we will promptly send you the practice tests.

Utilizing the Practice Tests
Setting Up Your Practice Environment:
1. Choose a quiet, comfortable space where you will not be disturbed.
2. Gather all necessary materials, including a calculator, scratch paper, and writing utensils.
3. Set a timer to replicate the actual test duration for each section.

Taking the Test:
1. Download and print the practice test, or complete it on your device if you prefer.
2. Follow the instructions and timing guidelines closely to simulate real test conditions.
3. Take the test in one sitting, with short breaks as outlined in the actual test schedule.

Reviewing Your Answers:
1. After completing the test, use the provided answer key to score your test.
2. Carefully review the detailed explanations for each question, noting areas where you made mistakes.
3. Identify patterns in your errors to focus your study efforts on specific topics or question types.

Tracking Your Progress:
1. Use a notebook or digital document to track your scores and note areas for improvement.
2. Periodically retake the exams simulations to assess your development and modify your study schedule as necessary.

Active Learning:
1. Engage in active reading and note-taking while reviewing explanations and study materials.
2. Make your own flashcards for easy review after summarizing ideas.
3. Form a study group with peers preparing for the Digital SAT®. Discussing questions and explanations can provide new insights and improve understanding.
4. Integrate practice tests into your regular study routine. Once the exam day draws near, try to finish one full-length examination every week at the latest.

An essential component of your preparation for the Digital SAT® is the five full-length PDF practice exams. They offer an accurate representation of the testing environment, support the development of test-taking endurance, and provide insightful feedback on your performance. Through consistent practice with these exams and making use of the thorough explanations and answer keys, you will be able to pinpoint your areas of weakness, monitor your improvement, and eventually improve your score on the Digital SAT®.

Recall that the secret to success is constant, concentrated practice coupled with a deep comprehension of the structure and subject matter of the test. Make use of the available materials, maintain a disciplined study schedule, and approach the Digital SAT® with assurance. Through the use of these thorough practice exams, you may hone your abilities and improve your score, putting you in a position to succeed academically.

CHAPTER 19: CONCLUSION

It's critical to keep in mind that attitude and mindset are just as important to success on the Digital SAT® as knowledge and practice are. This road you are on is more than just a means of getting to college; it is evidence of your commitment, tenacity, and drive. As you approach this momentous day, let's concentrate on the traits and techniques that will help you overcome not only the SAT® but all of life's obstacles.

The first step to passing the Digital SAT® is realizing how difficult the test is. Take the challenge as an opportunity to prove your skills, knowledge, and growth as a person. Every practice session, error, and achievement is a step closer to mastery. Recall that challenges are chances to grow and learn rather than impediments.

Your performance is greatly influenced by your thinking. Have an optimistic outlook on both your study and the test itself. Replace self-doubting ideas with positive ones that reassure you of your preparation and capability. Imagine yourself succeeding, appearing confident as you enter the testing facility and providing precise answers to questions. Your performance can be considerably improved by this mental practice.

To be resilient is to be able to bounce back from adversity.. You can run upon challenging material or practice tests that don't go as planned Consider these times as teaching opportunities rather than as a reason to give up. Examine your blunders, determine what went wrong, and devise plans of action to steer clear of the same mistakes in the future. Not only can resilience benefit you on the SAT®, but it will also be extremely useful in your academic and career endeavors.

Although stress is a normal part of getting ready, it doesn't have to be harmful. Discover effective stress-reduction techniques, such as regular exercise, deep breathing, and mindfulness. By keeping your mind clear and concentrated, these techniques can help you give your best work. Recall that part of a well-rounded preparation strategy also includes making sure you get enough sleep and taking breaks.

You are not alone on this trip. Rely on your network of friends and family for assistance. Discuss your objectives and difficulties with them. Their support and guidance might give you the inspiration and outlook you need to stay on course. An encouraging word or an alternative perspective can sometimes make all the difference.

Organization and consistency are essential for efficient planning. Make a study plan that will allow you to finish all of the material in a timely manner and allow time for review and practice exams. Evaluate your development and modify your plan as needed. Maintaining organization helps you feel less stressed at the last minute and guarantees that you are ready for every test section.

Along the journey, acknowledge and appreciate your accomplishments. Reaching a higher score on a practice test or grasping a challenging subject are examples of minor victories that bring you closer to your final objective. Honoring these achievements keeps you inspired and strengthens your confidence in your capacity for success. Give your success some thought. Imagine being pleased with yourself after learning your SAT® results. Imagine yourself beginning this exciting new chapter of your life by being admitted into the college of your dreams. You can use visualization as a very effective method to stay motivated and goal-focused.

Your success is fueled by your unwavering dedication to your objectives. Remind yourself of your goals and the reason you embarked on this road. Not only will your SAT® scores improve as a result of your commitment and hard effort, but your academic and career goals will also benefit from it.

Lastly, accept the adventure as it is. The test result is not as valuable as the preparatory procedure. You are strengthening your critical thinking abilities, learning efficient time management techniques, and establishing the discipline that will serve you well in college and beyond during this journey. Accept each day as it comes, develop from it all, and be proud of your progress. As you wrap up this preparatory guide, keep in mind that you already possess all the resources and techniques you require for success. Have a positive outlook, resilience, and confidence when taking the Digital SAT®. Have confidence in your own skills and potential for success.

The future is bright, and you will have countless opportunities thanks to your diligence and perseverance. Move forth with assurance and leave your imprint. The world is eager for the special contributions that you alone are capable of making. Wishing you luck and a successful and fulfilling path ahead.

DOWNLOAD YOUR FREE BONUS

We have some exclusive bonus materials for you as a way of saying thank you and to further enhance your experience. These extras include:

- **BONUS 1: Advanced Memorization Strategies**
- **BONUS 2: Anxiety Management - Techniques for Maintaining Calm and Focus**
- **BONUS 3: Strategies For Mastering The Digital Sat®**

To claim these valuable resources go to:

<u>https://publishingltd.my.canva.site/digital-sat</u>

Or scan the QR code provided below with your smartphone or tablet.

If you need support to download your bonuses for free or have any questions or suggestions, contact us at <u>publishingltd@outlook.com</u>

We will be happy to assist you!

Made in the USA
Las Vegas, NV
02 August 2024

93278482R00072